JOHN ASHBERY was born in Rochester, New York, in 1927 and grew up on a farm near Lake Ontario. He took a B.A. at Harvard in 1949 and in 1955 received a Fulbright Scholarship to study in France. Subsequently he lived there for ten years, mostly in Paris; from 1960 to 1965 he was art critic for the Paris edition of the *New York Herald Tribune*. He also helped edit a literary review called *Art and Literature*. Since 1965 he has lived in New York, and he is an editor of *Art News*. His poetry books include *Some Trees* (1956), *The Tennis Court Oath* (1962), *Rivers and Mountains* (1966), *The Double Dream of Spring* (1970) and *Selected Poems*, published in England in 1967. He is co-author with James Schuyler of a humorous novel called *A Nest of Ninnies* (1969).

LEE HARWOOD was born in 1939 in Leicester and raised in Chertsey and East London. Since 1963 he has edited several 'little magazines' and given poetry readings around England and the U.S.A. In between travelling and writing, his jobs include working as a stone-mason, librarian, bookseller, forester and bus-conductor. In 1966 he received the Poetry Foundation (New York) annual award. His books are: '*title illegible*' (1965), *The Man with Blue Eyes* (1966), *The White Room* (1968), *The Beautiful Atlas* (1969), *Landscapes* (1969), and *The Sinking Colony* (1970). He has also translated work by Tristan Tzara and published *Tristan Tzara – Cosmic Realities Vanilla Tobacco Dawnings*. An LP record of Lee Harwood reading his own poems is entitled *Landscapes*.

TOM RAWORTH was born in 1938. Between 1959 and 1967 he edited the magazine *Outburst* and founded two presses: first Matrix, and then, with Barry Hall, Goliard. From 1969 to 1970 he was resident poet in the literature department of the University of Essex. His books are *The Relation Ship* (1966), which was awarded the Alice Hunt Bartlett Prize for 1969, *Haiku* (1968, with John Esam and Anselm Hollo), *The Big Green Day* (1968), *A Serial Biography* (1969, prose), *Lion Lion* (1970), *Moving* (1971), and *Nicht Wahr, Rosie?* (1971).

Penguin Modern Poets

19

JOHN ASHBERY

LEE HARWOOD

TOM RAWORTH

Penguin Books

Penguin Books Ltd, Harmondsworth, Middlesex, England
Penguin Books Inc., 7110 Ambassador Road, Baltimore, Maryland 21207, U.S.A.
Penguin Books Australia Ltd, Ringwood, Victoria, Australia

—

This selection first published 1971

—

Copyright © Penguin Books Ltd, 1971

—

Made and printed in Great Britain by
Cox & Wyman Ltd, London, Reading and Fakenham
Set in Monotype Garamond

Contents

CONTENTS

CONTENTS

Acknowledgements

THE poems by John Ashbery are taken from *Some Trees*, in the Yale Series of Younger Poets, copyright © by John Ashbery; *Rivers and Mountains*, copyright © 1962, 1963, 1964, 1966 by John Ashbery, reprinted by permission of Holt, Rinehart and Winston, Inc.; *The Double Dream of Spring*, 1970, published by E. P. Dutton & Co. Inc.; and *The Tennis Court Oath*, 1962, published by Wesleyan University Press, copyright © 1959, 1960, 1961, 1962 by John Ashbery. Reprinted from *The Tennis Court Oath*, by John Ashbery, by permission of Wesleyan University Press. 'Popular Songs', 'Sonnet', 'And You Know', 'They Dream Only of America', 'A Last World', 'Rivers and Mountains', and 'A Blessing in Disguise' are reprinted from *Selected Poems*, 1967, by permission of Jonathan Cape Ltd.

The poems by Lee Harwood are taken from *White Room*, copyright © Lee Harwood, 1968, *Landscapes*, copyright © Lee Harwood, 1969, and *The Sinking Colony*, copyright © Lee Harwood, 1970, all published by Fulcrum Press, by whose permission the poems are reprinted. Five poems from *White Room* also appear in *The Man with Blue Eyes*, 1966, published by Angel Hair Books, New York. The poem 'inside the harm is a clearing . . .' is from *The Big Chop*, to be published in 1971 by Fulcrum Press.

The poems by Tom Raworth are from *The Relation Ship*, copyright © Tom Raworth, 1966, 1969, and *Moving*,

ACKNOWLEDGEMENTS

to be published in 1971, both by Cape Goliard Press; *The Big Green Day*, 1968, *Haiku*, 1968, and *Lion Lion*, 1970, all published by Trigram Press; and from *Nicht Wahr, Rosie?*, copyright © Tom Raworth, 1971, published by Fulcrum Press.

JOHN ASHBERY

Two Scenes

I

We see us as we truly behave:
From every corner comes a distinctive offering.
The train comes bearing joy;
The sparks it strikes illuminate the table.
Destiny guides the water-pilot, and it is destiny.
For long we hadn't heard so much news, such noise.
The day was warm and pleasant.
'We see you in your hair,
Air resting around the tips of mountains.'

II

A fine rain anoints the canal machinery.
This is perhaps a day of general honesty
Without example in the world's history
Though the fumes are not of a singular authority
And indeed are dry as poverty.
Terrific units are on an old man
In the blue shadow of some paint cans
As laughing cadets say, 'In the evening
Everything has a schedule, if you **can** **find** **out** what it is.'

Popular Songs

He continued to consult her for her beauty
(The host gone to a longing grave).
The story then resumed in day coaches
Both bravely eyed the finer dust on the blue. That
    summer
('The worst ever') she stayed in the car with the cur.
That was something between her legs.
Alton had been getting letters from his mother
About the payments – half the flood
Over and what about the net rest of the year?
Who cares? Anyway (you know how thirsty they
    were)
The extra worry began it – on the
Blue blue mountain – she never set foot
And then and there. Meanwhile the host
Mourned her quiet tenure. They all stayed chatting.
No one did much about eating.
The tears came and stopped, came and stopped, until
Becoming the guano-lightened summer night
    landscape,
All one glow, one mild laugh lasting ages.
Some precision, he fumed into his soup.

You laugh. There is no peace in the fountain.
The footmen smile and shift. The mountain
Rises nightly to disappointed stands
Dining in 'The Gardens of the Moon'.
There is no way to prevent this
Or the expectation of disappointment.
All are aware, some carry a secret

Better, of hands emulating deeds
Of days untrustworthy. But these may decide.
The face extended its sorrowing light
Far out over them. And now silent as a group
The actors prepare their first decline.

The Grapevine

Of who we and all they are
You all now know. But you know
After they began to find us out we grew
Before they died thinking us the causes

Of their acts. Now we'll not know
The truth of some still at the piano, though
They often date from us, causing
These changes we think we are. We don't care

Though, so tall up there
In young air. But things get darker as we move
To ask them: Whom must we get to know
To die, so you live and we know?

Glazunoviana

The man with the red hat
And the polar bear, is he here too?
The window giving on shade,
Is that here too?
And all the little helps,
My initials in the sky,
The hay of an arctic summer night?

The bear
Drops dead in sight of the window.
Lovely tribes have just moved to the north.
In the flickering evening the martins grow denser.
Rivers of wings surround us and vast tribulation.

Sonnet

Each servant stamps the reader with a look.
After many years he has been brought nothing.
The servant's frown is the reader's patience.
The servant goes to bed.
The patience rambles on
Musing on the library's lofty holes.

His pain is the servant's alive.
It pushes to the top stain of the wall
Its tree-top's head of excitement:
Baskets, birds, beetles, spools.
The light walls collapse next day.
Traffic is the reader's pictured face.
Dear, be the tree your sleep awaits;
Worms be your words, you not safe from ours.

And You Know

The girls, protected by gold wire from the gaze
Of the onrushing students, live in an atmosphere of vacuum
In the old schoolhouse covered with nasturtiums.
At night, comets, shooting stars, twirling planets,
Suns, bits of illuminated pumice, and spooks hang over the old
    place;
The atmosphere is breathless. Some find the summer light
Nauseous and damp, but there are those
Who are charmed by it, going out into the morning.
We must rest here, for this is where the teacher comes.
On his desk stands a vase of tears.
A quiet feeling pervades the playroom. His voice clears
Through the interminable afternoon: 'I was a child once
Under the spangled sun. Now I do what must be done.
I teach reading and writing and flaming arithmetic. Those
In my home come to me anxiously at night, asking how it
    goes.
My door is always open. I never lie, and the great heat warms
    me.'

His door is always open, the fond schoolmaster!
We ought to imitate him in our lives,
For as a man lives, he dies. To pass away
In the afternoon, on the vast vapid bank
You think is coming to crown you with hollyhocks and
    lilacs, or in gold at the opera,
Requires that one shall have lived so much! And not merely
Asking questions and giving answers, but grandly sitting,
Like a great rock, through many years.
It is the erratic path of time we trace

On the globe, with moist fingertip, and surely, the globe
    stops;
We are pointing to England, to Africa, to Nigeria;
And we shall visit these places, you and I, and other
    places,
Including heavenly Naples, queen of the sea, where I shall
    be king and you will be queen,
And all the places around Naples.
So the good old teacher is right, to stop with his finger on
    Naples, gazing out into the mild December afternoon
As his star pupil enters the classroom in that elaborate
    black-and-yellow creation.
He is thinking of her flounces, and is caught in them as
    if they were made of iron, they will crush him to
    death!
Good-bye, old teacher, we must travel on, not to a better
    land, perhaps,
But to the England of the sonnets, Paris, Colombia, and
    Switzerland
And all the places with names, that we wish to visit –
    Strasbourg, Albania,
The coast of Holland, Madrid, Singapore, Naples, Salonika,
    Liberia, and Turkey.
So we leave you behind with her of the black-and-yellow
    flounces.
You were always a good friend, but a special one.
Now as we brush through the clinging leaves we seem to
    hear you crying;
You want us to come back, but it is too late to come back,
    isn't it?
It is too late to go to the places with the names (what were
    they, anyway? just names).
It is too late to go anywhere but to the nearest star, that one,
    that hangs just over the hill, beckoning

Like a hand of which the arm is not visible. Good-bye,
   Father! Good-bye, pupils. Good-bye, my master and my
   dame.
We fly to the nearest star, whether it be red like a furnace, or
   yellow,
And we carry your lessons in our hearts (the lessons and our
   hearts are the same)
Out of the humid classroom, into the forever. Good-bye,
   Old Dog Tray.

And so they have left us feeling tired and old.
They never cared for school anyway.
And they have left us with the things pinned on the bulletin
   board,
And the night, the endless, muggy night that is invading
   our school.

'They Dream Only of America'

They dream only of America
To be lost among the thirteen million pillars of grass:
'This honey is delicious
Though it burns the throat.'

And hiding from darkness in barns
They can be grownups now
And the murderer's ash tray is more easily –
The lake a lilac cube.

He holds a key in his right hand.
'Please,' he asked willingly.
He is thirty years old.
That was before

We could drive hundreds of miles
At night through dandelions.
When his headache grew worse we
Stopped at a wire filling station.

Now he cared only about signs.
Was the cigar a sign?
And what about the key?
He went slowly into the bedroom.

'I would not have broken my leg if I had not fallen
Against the living room table. What is it to be back
Beside the bed? There is nothing to do
For our liberation, except wait in the horror of it.

And I am lost without you.'

'How Much Longer Will I Be Able to Inhabit the Divine Sepulcher . . .'

How much longer will I be able to inhabit the divine
    sepulcher
Of life, my great love? Do dolphins plunge bottomward
To find the light? Or is it rock
That is searched? Unrelentingly? Huh. And if some day

Men with orange shovels come to break open the rock
Which encases me, what about the light that comes in then?
What about the smell of the light?
What about the moss?

In pilgrim times he wounded me
Since then I only lie
My bed of light is a furnace choking me
With hell (and sometimes I hear salt water dripping).

I mean it – because I'm one of the few
To have held my breath under the house. I'll trade
One red sucker for two blue ones. I'm
Named Tom. The

Light bounces off mossy rocks down to me
In this glen (the neat villa! which
When he'd had he would not had he of
And jests smarting of privet

Which on hot spring nights perfumes the empty rooms
With the smell of sperm flushed down toilets
On hot summer afternoons within sight of the sea.
If you knew why then professor) reads

To his friends: Drink to me only with
And the reader is carried away
By a great shadow under the sea.
Behind the steering wheel

The boy took out his own forehead.
His girlfriend's head was a green bag
Of narcissus stems. 'OK you win
But meet me anyway at Cohen's Drug Store

In 22 minutes.' What a marvel is ancient man!
Under the tulip roots he has figured out a way to be a
    religious animal
And would be a mathematician. But where in unsuitable
    heaven
Can he get the heat that will make him grow?

For he needs something or will forever remain a dwarf,
Though a perfect one, and possessing a normal-sized brain
But he has got to be released by giants from things.
And as the plant grows older it realizes it will never be
    a tree,

Will probably always be haunted by a bee
And cultivates stupid impressions
So as not to become part of the dirt. The dirt
Is mounting like a sea. And we say good-bye

Shaking hands in front of the crashing of the waves
That give our words lonesomeness, and make these flabby
    hands seem ours —
Hands that are always writing things
On mirrors for people to see later —

Do you want them to water
Plant, tear listlessly among the exchangeable ivy –
Carrying food to mouth, touching genitals –
But no doubt you have understood

It all now and I am a fool. It remains
For me to get better, and to understand you so
Like a chair-sized man. Boots
Were heard on the floor above. In the garden the sunlight
    was still purple

But what buzzed in it had changed slightly
But not forever . . . but casting its shadow
On sticks, and looking around for an opening in the air, was
    quite as if it had never refused to exist differently. Guys
In the yard handled the belt he had made

Stars
Painted the garage roof crimson and black
He is not a man
Who can read these signs . . . his bones were stays . . .

And even refused to live
In a world and refunded the hiss
Of all that exists terribly near us
Like you, my love, and light.

For what is obedience but the air around us
To the house? For which the federal men came
In a minute after the sidewalk
Had taken you home? ('Latin . . . blossom . . .')

After which you led me to water
And bade me drink, which I did, owing to your kindness.

You would not let me out for two days and three nights,
Bringing me books bound in wild thyme and scented wild
    grasses

As if reading had any interest for me, you ...
Now you are laughing.
Darkness interrupts my story.
Turn on the light.

Meanwhile what am I going to do?
I am growing up again, in school, the crisis will be very soon.
And you twist the darkness in your fingers, you
Who are slightly older ...

Who are you, anyway?
And it is the color of sand,
The darkness, as it sifts through your hand
Because what does anything mean,

The ivy and the sand? That boat
Pulled up on the shore? Am I wonder,
Strategically, and in the light
Of the long sepulcher that hid death and hides me?

An Additional Poem

Where then shall hope and fear their objects find?
The harbor cold to the mating ships,
And you have lost as you stand by the balcony
With the forest of the sea calm and gray beneath.
A strong impression torn from the descending light
But night is guilty. You knew the shadow
In the trunk was raving
But as you keep growing hungry you forget.
The distant box is open. A sound of grain
Poured over the floor in some eagerness – we
Rise with the night let out of the box of wind.

Thoughts of a Young Girl

'It is such a beautiful day I had to write you a letter
From the tower, and to show I'm not mad:
I only slipped on the cake of soap of the air
And drowned in the bathtub of the world.
You were too good to cry much over me.
And now I let you go. Signed, The Dwarf.'

I passed by late in the afternoon
And the smile still played about her lips
As it has for centuries. She always knows
How to be utterly delightful. Oh my daughter,
My sweetheart, daughter of my late employer, princess,
May you not be long on the way!

Faust

If only the phantom would stop reappearing!
Business, if you wanted to know, was punk at the opera.
The heroine no longer appeared in *Faust*.
The crowds strolled sadly away. The phantom
Watched them from the roof, not guessing the hungers
That must be stirred before disappointment can begin.

One day as morning was about to begin
A man in brown with a white shirt reappearing
At the bottom of his yellow vest, was talking hungers
With the silver-haired director of the opera.
On the green-carpeted floor no phantom
Appeared, except yellow squares of sunlight, like those in
    Faust.

That night as the musicians for *Faust*
Were about to go on strike, lest darkness begin
In the corridors, and through them the phantom
Glide unobstructed, the vision reappearing
Of blonde Marguerite practicing a new opera
At her window awoke terrible new hungers

In the already starving tenor. But hungers
Are just another topic, like the new Faust
Drifting through the tunnels of the opera
(In search of lost old age? For they begin
To notice a twinkle in his eye. It is cold daylight reappearing
At the window behind him, itself a phantom

Window, painted by the phantom
Scene painters, sick of not getting paid, of hungers

For a scene below of tiny, reappearing
Dancers, with a sandbag falling like a note in *Faust*
Through purple air. And the spectators begin
To understand the bleeding tenor star of the opera.)

That night the opera
Was crowded to the rafters. The phantom
Took twenty-nine curtain calls. 'Begin!
Begin!' In the wings the tenor hungers
For the heroine's convulsive kiss, and Faust
Moves forward, no longer young, reappearing

And reappearing for the last time. The opera
Faust would no longer need its phantom.
On the bare, sunlit stage the hungers could begin.

A Last World

These wonderful things
Were planted on the surface of a round mind that was to
    become our present time.
The mark of things belongs to someone
But if that somebody was wise
Then the whole of things might be different
From what it was thought to be in the beginning, before an
    angel bandaged the field glasses.
Then one could say nothing hear nothing
Of what the great time spoke to its divisors.
All borders between men were closed.
Now all is different without having changed
As though one were to pass through the same street at
    different times
And nothing that is old can prefer the new.
An enormous merit has been placed on the head of all things
Which, bowing down, arrive near the region of their feet
So that the earth-stone has stared at them in memory at the
    approach of an error.
Still it is not too late for these things to die
Provided that an anemone will grab them and rush them to
    the wildest heaven.
But having plucked oneself, who could live in the sunlight?
And the truth is cold, as a giant's knee
Will seem cold.

Yet having once played with tawny truth
Having once looked at a cold mullet on a plate on a table
    supported by the weight of the inconstant universe
He wished to go far away from himself.

There were no baskets in those jovial pine-tree forests, and
    the waves pushed without whitecaps
In that foam where he wished to be.

Man is never without woman, the neuter sex
Casting up her equations, looks to her lord for loving
    kindness
For man smiles never at woman.
In the forests a night landslide could disclose that she smiled.
Guns were fired to discourage dogs into the interior
But woman – never. She is completely out of this world.
She climbs a tree to see if he is coming
Sunlight breaks at the edge of the wet lakes
And she is happy, if free
For the power he forces down at her like a storm of lightning.

Once a happy old man
One can never change the core of things, and light burns you
    the harder for it.
Glad of the changes already and if there are more it will never
    be you that minds
Since it will not be you to be changed, but in the evening in
    the severe lamplight doubts come
From many scattered distances, and do not come too near.
As it falls along the house, your treasure
Cries to the other men; the darkness will have none of you,
    and you are folded into it like mint into the sound of
    haying.
It was ninety-five years ago that you strolled in the serene
    little port; under an enormous cornice six boys in black
    slowly stood.
Six frock coats today, six black fungi tomorrow,
And the day after tomorrow – but the day after tomorrow
    itself is blackening dust.

You court obsidian pools
And from a tremendous height twilight falls like a stone and
    hits you.

You who were always in the way
Flower
Are you afraid of trembling like breath
But there is no breath in seriousness; the lake howls for it.
Swiftly sky covers earth, the wrong breast for a child to
    suck, and that,
What have you got there in your hand?

It is a stone

So the passions are divided into tiniest units
And of these many are lost, and those that remain are given
    at nightfall to the uneasy old man
The old man who goes skipping along the roadbed.
In a dumb harvest
Passions are locked away, and states of creation are used
    instead, that is to say synonyms are used.

Honey
On the lips of elders is not contenting, so
A firebrand is made. Woman carries it,
She who thought herself good only for bearing children is
    decked out in the lace of fire
And this is exactly the way she wanted it, the trees coming
    to place themselves in her
In a rite of torpor, dust.
A bug carries the elixir
Naked men pray the ground and chew it with their hands
The fire lives
Men are nabbed

She her bonnet half off is sobbing there while the massacre
    yet continues with a terrific thin energy
A silver blaze calms the darkness.

Rest undisturbed on the dry of the beach
Flower
And night stand suddenly sideways to observe your bones
Vixen

Do men later go home
Because we wanted to travel
Under the kettle of trees
We thought the sky would melt to receive us
But to tell the truth the air turned to smoke,
We were forced back onto a foul pillow that was another
    place
Or were lost by our comrades
Somewhere between heaven and no place, and were growing
    smaller.
In another place a mysterious mist shot up like a wall, down
    which trickled the tears of our loved ones.
Bananas rotten with their ripeness hung from the leaves,
    and cakes and jewels covered the sand.
But these were not the best men
But there were moments of the others
Seen through indifference, only bare methods
But we can remember them and so we are saved.

A last world moves on the figures;
They are smaller than when we last saw them caring about
    them.
The sky is a giant rocking horse
And of the other things death is a new office building filled
    with modern furniture,

A wise thing, but which has no purpose for us.

Everything is being blown away;
A little horse trots up with a letter in its mouth, which is
    read with eagerness
As we gallop into the flame.

Idaho

During the past few months, Biff had become quite a frequent visitor to Carol's apartment.

He never failed to marvel at the cool, corrected elegance of the place as contrasted with its warm, rippling, honey-blonde occupant. The apothecary jars,

Chippendale furniture,

and wall-to-wall carpeting were strangely out of keeping with Carol's habitual 'Hiya good lookin'' as she came forward to greet him, wrapped in one of those big fuzzy bathrobes and drying her hair on a Turkish towel. Or were his calculations somehow awry? Was there, deep within this warm, vital-seeming presence a steel vein so thin as to be almost invisible? Or was this, too, a mistake?

Their whole conduct had been, up to now, not impersonal exactly, but utterly devoid of any recognition of sex-consciousness. In conversation they had 'swapped backgrounds', as Biff called it. Carol, her eyes wet with tears at the picture of his isolation in the crowded rectory, had uttered a deep sigh at her own recital of being left for the first eight years of her life to the sole care of Patches.

With the unconscious dramatic heightening that always goes with a sympathetic audience, each of them, intensely serious and really moved, had lifted corners of the veil for the other to peep through. They had been very close to each other in attention, in sympathy, in response, but with none of the subtle emphasis which marks the recognized intrusion of sex. Carol was aware today, however, that Biff had suddenly become obsessed with a sense of her: that he had caught fire. She was aware of vast excitement,

apprehension,

a mental

'Can I give you a hand?'
She gave a little cry that was silenced by mouth on
uttermost tingling nerve
'Carol!' he said. Can this be the one time
?????????????????????????
She had known how from

Biff: The last Rhode Island reds are
'diet of hamburgers and orange juice'

Exactly what kind of perfection?????????????????????????
I see into fields of timothy
one
the others   time
change

,,,,,,,and they walked back,
small hand-assemblies

'What does it mean??????????????'

Carol laughed. Among other things,
till I've finished it. It's the reason of
dropped into Brentano's.
get some of the
a pile of these. I just grabbed one . . .
– Oh, by the way, there's a tele-
'See?' She pointed to the table.
Cornelia unfolded the piece of crude blue paper that is a French
telegra.
#############
The mouth of weeds

marriage.' She shivered. 'It's – it's a death!'

II

The door of the studio slammed.
'Hullo, honey!' Cornelia said.
was the last practical   from now on, whispers
leading into the night

flowers, moral turpitude,
She had had more than enough. Why, in Stone Age
vessels
But that doesn't explain. Her mind opened it-
Every tendril of thought,,,,,,,,,,,
It sees through a magnifying glass
genius
a special aureole
Niagara of affliction.   had learned this
heard it
into the
window the long platform at Oxford, and Carol
lowered the
When the train stopped the army
You had nothing about it. That's no Bob!!!!!!!!!!!!!!!!!!

A whistle blew shrilly
the slow evening
silver note
the main road automobiles
majestic stag-beetles, with a high, sweet hum
that moment for long
thoughts and low red voices
the mood was shattered
'twenty-seven'   Just as that act changes
nerve-centers
birthdays –

She rose from the table abruptly. 'You must smoke your cigar alone tonight. I – I'm going out in the car. She went upstairs and changed into a different pair of shoes

and a sweater.

Jim was pouring himself another glass of port as she came down.

'''''''''' 'I won't be very long,'''''''''' she said. ⌗⌗⌗⌗⌗⌗⌗⌗

nodded. 'Take care of yourself.' She closed the door behind her and went

down through

the garden. A carnation struck her hand as she passed. She picked it,

sniffed deeply, and put the stalk in her mouth. 'Twenty-seven! Twenty-seven!' She went into the garage, a little house of wood, tucked into the bank at the edge of the road. It was Jim's car, a present from Carol. She had earned it in the year

following the exhibition, had learned to drive it at an automobile school in London, and had a special low bunk designed for Jim alongside the driver's seat. The carnation made a crimson

splash against her cheek as she drove out

and headed down the hill towards the main road. Up in the cottage Patches 'Good 'eavens! Is that

> For who dies
> The crocus ideally
> On life's playing field
> The 'never mind' rubbish
> All, all fixed
> running water
> And the proper names,
> blood out of courage
> to fix

to feel
the stem of air

great, senseless knob
brownies ahead and the clutch. 'Twenty-seven! Twenty-seven!'
sniffed loudly
the car window
listening car had ceased.

A whistle blew shrilly.

These Lacustrine Cities

These lacustrine cities grew out of loathing
Into something forgetful, although angry with history.
They are the product of an idea: that man is horrible, for
    instance,
Though this is only one example.

They emerged until a tower
Controlled the sky, and with artifice dipped back
Into the past for swans and tapering branches,
Burning, until all that hate was transformed into useless love.

Then you are left with an idea of yourself
And the feeling of ascending emptiness of the afternoon
Which must be charged to the embarrassment of others
Who fly by you like beacons.

The night is a sentinel.
Much of your time has been occupied by creative games
Until now, but we have all-inclusive plans for you.
We had thought, for instance, of sending you to the middle
    of the desert,

To a violent sea, or of having the closeness of the others be air
To you, pressing you back into a startled dream
As sea-breezes greet a child's face.
But the past is already here, and you are nursing some private
    project.

The worst is not over, yet I know
You will be happy here. Because of the logic
Of your situation, which is something no climate can
     outsmart.
Tender and insouciant by turns, you see

You have built a mountain of something,
Thoughtfully pouring all your energy into this single
     monument,
Whose wind is desire starching a petal,
Whose disappointment broke into a rainbow of tears.

Rivers and Mountains

On the secret map the assassins
Cloistered, the Moon River was marked
Near the eighteen peaks and the city
Of humiliation and defeat – wan ending
Of the trail among dry, papery leaves
Gray-brown quills like thoughts
In the melodious but vast mass of today's
Writing through fields and swamps
Marked, on the map, with little bunches of weeds.
Certainly squirrels lived in the woods
But devastation and dull sleep still
Hung over the land, quelled
The rioters turned out of sleep in the peace of prisons
Singing on marble factory walls
Deaf consolation of minor tunes that pack
The air with heavy invisible rods
Pent in some sand valley from
Which only quiet walking ever instructs.
The bird flew over and
Sat – there was nothing else to do.
Do not mistake its silence for pride or strength
Or the waterfall for a harbor
Full of light boats that is there
Performing for thousands of people
In clothes some with places to go
Or games. Sometimes over the pillar
Of square stones its impact
Makes a light print.

So going around cities
To get to other places you found

It all on paper but the land
Was made of paper processed
To look like ferns, mud or other
Whose sea unrolled its magic
Distances and then rolled them up
Its secret was only a pocket
After all but some corners are darker
Than these moonless nights spent as on a raft
In the seclusion of a melody heard
As though through trees
And you can never ignite their touch
Long but there were homes
Flung far out near the asperities
Of a sharp, rocky pinnacle
And other collective places
Shadows of vineyards whose wine
Tasted of the forest floor
Fisheries and oyster beds
Tides under the pole
Seminaries of instruction, public
Places for electric light
And the major tax assessment area
Wrinkled on the plan
Of election to public office
Sixty-two years old bath and breakfast
The formal traffic, shadows
To make it not worth joining
After the ox had pulled away the cart.

Your plan was to separate the enemy into two groups
With the razor-edged mountains between.
It worked well on paper
But their camp had grown
To be the mountains and the map

46

Carefully peeled away and not torn
Was the light, a tender but tough bark
On everything. Fortunately the war was solved
In another way by isolating the two sections
Of the enemy's navy so that the mainland
Warded away the big floating ships.
Light bounced off the ends
Of the small gray waves to tell
Them in the observatory
About the great drama that was being won
To turn off the machinery
And quietly move among the rustic landscape
Scooping snow off the mountains rinsing
The coarser ones that love had
Slowly risen in the night to overflow
Wetting pillow and petal
Determined to place the letter
On the unassassinated president's desk
So that a stamp could reproduce all this
In detail, down to the last autumn leaf
And the affliction of June ride
Slowly out into the sun-blackened landscape.

Last Month

No changes of support – only
Patches of gray, here where sunlight fell.
The house seems heavier
Now that they have gone away.
In fact it emptied in record time.
When the flat table used to result
A match recedes, slowly, into the night.
The academy of the future is
Opening its doors and willing
The fruitless sunlight streams into domes
The chairs piled high with books and papers.

The sedate one is this month's skittish one
Confirming the property that,
A timeless value, has changed hands.
And you could have a new automobile
Ping pong set and garage, but the thief
Stole everything like a miracle.
In his book there was a picture of treason only
And in the garden, cries and colors.

A Blessing in Disguise

Yes, they are alive and can have those colors,
But I, in my soul, am alive too.
I feel I must sing and dance, to tell
Of this in a way, that knowing you may be drawn to me.

And I sing amid despair and isolation
Of the chance to know you, to sing of me
Which are you. You see,
You hold me up to the light in a way

I should never have expected, or suspected, perhaps
Because you always tell me I am you,
And right. The great spruces loom.
I am yours to die with, to desire.

I cannot ever think of me, I desire you
For a room in which the chairs ever
Have their backs turned to the light
Inflicted on the stone and paths, the real trees

That seem to shine at me through a lattice toward you.
If the wild light of this January day is true
I pledge me to be truthful unto you
Whom I cannot ever stop remembering.

Remembering to forgive. Remember to pass beyond you
        into the day
On the wings of the secret you will never know.
Taking me from myself, in the path
Which the pastel girth of the day has assigned to me.

I prefer 'you' in the plural, I want 'you',
You must come to me, all golden and pale
Like the dew and the air.
And then I start getting this feeling of exaltation.

Clepsydra

Hasn't the sky? Returned from moving the other
Authority recently dropped, wrested as much of
That severe sunshine as you need now on the way
You go. The reason why it happened only since
You woke up is letting the steam disappear
From those clouds when the landscape all around
Is hilly sites that will have to be reckoned
Into the total for there to be more air: that is,
More fitness read into the undeduced result, than land.
This means never getting any closer to the basic
Principle operating behind it than to the distracted
Entity of a mirage. The half-meant, half-perceived
Motions of fronds out of idle depths that are
Summer. And expansion into little draughts.
The reply wakens easily, darting from
Untruth to willed moment, scarcely called into being
Before it swells, the way a waterfall
Drums at different levels. Each moment
Of utterance is the true one; likewise none are true,
Only is the bounding from air to air, a serpentine
Gesture which hides the truth behind a congruent
Message, the way air hides the sky, is, in fact,
Tearing it limb from limb this very moment: but
The sky has pleaded already and this is about
As graceful a kind of non-absence as either
Has a right to expect: whether it's the form of
Some creator who has momentarily turned away,
Marrying detachment with respect, so that the pieces
Are seen as parts of a spectrum, independent
Yet symbolic of their spaced-out times of arrival;

Whether on the other hand all of it is to be
Seen as no luck. A recurring whiteness like
The face of stone pleasure, urging forward as
Nostrils what only meant dust. But the argument,
That is its way, has already left these behind: it
Is, it would have you believe, the white din up ahead
That matters: unformed yells, rocketings,
Affected turns, and tones of voice called
By upper shadows toward some cloud of belief
Or its unstated circumference. But the light
Has already gone from there too and it may be that
It is lines contracting into a plane. We hear so much
Of its further action that at last it seems that
It is we, our taking it into account rather, that are
The reply that prompted the question, and
That the latter, like a person waking on a pillow
Has the sensation of having dreamt the whole thing,
Of returning to participate in that dream, until
The last word is exhausted; certainly this is
Peace of a sort, like nets drying in the sun,
That we must progress toward the whole thing
About an hour ago. As long as it is there
You will desire it as its tag of wall sinks
Deeper as though hollowed by sunlight that
Just fits over it; it is both mirage and the little
That was present, the miserable totality
Mustered at any given moment, like your eyes
And all they speak of, such as your hands, in lost
Accents beyond any dream of ever wanting them again.
To have this to be constantly coming back from –
Nothing more, really, than surprise at your absence
And preparing to continue the dialogue into
Those mysterious and near regions that are
Precisely the time of its being furthered.

Seeing it, as it was, dividing that time,
Casting colored paddles against the welter
Of a future of disunion just to abolish confusion
And permit level walks into the gaze of its standing
Around admiringly, it was then, that it was these
Moments that were the truth, although each tapered
Into the distant surrounding night. But
Wasn't it their blindness, instead, and wasn't this
The fact of being so turned in on each other that
Neither would ever see his way clear again? It
Did not stagger the imagination so long as it stayed
This way, comparable to exclusion from the light of the stars
That drenched every instant of that being, in an egoistic way,
As though their round time were only the reverse
Of some more concealable, vengeful purpose to become known
Once its result had more or less established
The look of the horizon. But the condition
Of those moments of timeless elasticity and blindness
Was being joined secretly so
That their paths would cross again and be separated
Only to join again in a final assumption rising like a shout
And be endless in the discovery of the declamatory
Nature of the distance traveled. All this is
Not without small variations and surprises, yet
An invisible fountain continually destroys and
    refreshes the previsions.
Then is their permanence merely a function of
The assurance with which it's understood, assurance
Which, you might say, goes a long way toward conditioning
Whatever result? But there was no statement
At the beginning. There was only a breathless waste,
A dumb cry shaping everything in projected
After-effects orphaned by playing the part intended for them,
Though one must not forget that the nature of this

Emptiness, these previsions,
Was that it could only happen here, on this page held
Too close to be legible, sprouting erasures, except that they
Ended everything in the transparent sphere of what was
Intended only a moment ago, spiraling further out, its
Gesture finally dissolving in the weather.
It was the long way back out of sadness
Of that first meeting: a half-triumph, an imaginary feeling
Which still protected its events and pauses, the way
A telescope protects its view of distant mountains
And all they include, the coming and going,
Moving correctly up to other levels, preparing to spend the
        night
There where the tiny figures halt as darkness comes on,
Beside some loud torrent in an empty yet personal
Landscape, which has the further advantage of being
What surrounds without insisting, the very breath so
Honorably offered, and accepted in the same spirit.
There was in fact pleasure in those high walls.
Each moment seemed to bore back into the centuries
For profit and manners, and an old way of looking that
Continually shaped those lips into a smile. Or it was
Like standing at the edge of a harbor early on a summer
        morning
With the discreet shadows cast by the water all around
And a feeling, again, of emptiness, but of richness in the way
The whole thing is organized, on what a miraculous scale,
Really what is meant by a human level, with the figures of giants
Not too much bigger than the men who have come to
        petition them:
A moment that gave not only itself, but
Also the means of keeping it, of not turning to dust
Or gestures somewhere up ahead
But of becoming complicated like the torrent

In new dark passages, tears and laughter which
Are a sign of life, of distant life in this case.
And yet, as always happens, there would come a moment when
Acts no longer sufficed and the calm
Of this true progression hardened into shreds
Of another kind of calm, returning to the conclusion, its
    premises
Undertaken before any formal agreement had been reached,
    hence
A writ that was the shadow of the colossal reason behind
    all this
Like a second, rigid body behind the one you know is yours.
And it was in vain that tears blotted the contract now, because
It had been freely drawn up and consented to as insurance
Against the very condition it was now so efficiently
Seeking to establish. It had reduced that other world,
The round one of the telescope, to a kind of very fine
    powder or dust
So small that space could not remember it.
Thereafter any signs of feeling were cut short by
The comfort and security, a certain elegance even,
Like the fittings of a ship, that are after all
The most normal things in the world. Yes, perhaps, but
    the words
'After all' are important for understanding the almost
Exaggerated strictness of the condition, and why, in spite of
    this,
It seemed the validity of the former continuing was
Not likely to be reinstated for a long time.
'After all,' that too might be possible, as indeed
All kinds of things are possible in the widening angle of
The day, as it comes to blush with pleasure and increase,
So that light sinks into itself, becomes dark and heavy
Like a surface stained with ink: there was something

Not quite good or correct about the way
Things were looking recently: hadn't the point
Of all this new construction been to provide
A protected medium for the exchanges each felt of such vital
Concern, and wasn't it now giving itself the airs of a palace?
And yet her hair had never been so long.
It was a feeling of well-being, if you will, as though a smallest
Distant impulse had rendered the whole surface ultra-sensitive
But its fierceness was still acquiescence
To the nature of this goodness already past
And it was a kind of sweet acknowledgment of how
The past is yours, to keep invisible if you wish
But also to make absurd elaborations with
And in this way prolong your dance of non-discovery
In brittle, useless architecture that is nevertheless
The map of your desires, irreproachable, beyond
Madness and the toe of approaching night, if only
You desire to arrange it this way. Your acts
Are sentinels against this quiet
Invasion. Long may you prosper, and may your years
Be the throes of what is even now exhausting itself
In one last effort to outwit us; it could only be a map
Of the world: in their defeat such peninsulas as become
Prolongations of our reluctance to approach, but also
Fine days on whose memorable successions of events
We shall be ever afterwards tempted to dwell. I am
Not speaking of a partially successful attempt to be
Opposite; anybody at all can read that page, it has only
To be thrust in front of him. I mean now something much
      broader,
The sum total of all the private aspects than can ever
Become legible in what is outside, as much in the rocks
And foliage as in the invisible look of the distant
Ether and in the iron fist that suddenly closes over your own.

I see myself in this totality, and meanwhile
I am only a transparent diagram, of manners and
Private words with the certainty of being about to fall.
And even this crumb of life I also owe to you
For being so close as to seal out knowledge of that other
Voluntary life, and so keep its root in darkness until your
Maturity when your hair will actually be the branches
Of a tree with the light pouring through them.
It intensifies echoes in such a way as to
Form a channel to absorb every correct motion.
In this way any direction taken was the right one,
Leading first to you, and through you to
Myself that is beyond you and which is the same thing as space,
That is the stammering vehicles that remain unknown,
Eating the sky in all sincerity because the difference
Can never be made up: therefore, why not examine the distance?
It seemed he had been repeating the same stupid phrase
Over and over throughout his life; meanwhile
Infant destinies had suavely matured; there was
To be a meeting or collection of them that very evening.
He was out of it of course for having lain happily awake
On the tepid fringes of that field or whatever
Whose center was beginning to churn darkly, but even more
        for having
The progression of minutes by accepting them, as one accepts
        drops of rain
As they form a shower, and without worrying about the fine
        weather that will come after.
Why shouldn't all climate and all music be equal
Without growing? There should be an invariable balance of
Contentment to hold everything in place, ministering
To stunted memories, helping them stand alone
And return into the world, without ever looking back at
What they might have become, even though in doing so they

Might just once have been the truth that, invisible,
Still surrounds us like the air and is the dividing force
Between our slightest steps and the notes taken on them.
It is because everything is relative
That we shall never see in that sphere of pure wisdom and
Entertainment much more than groping shadows of an
    incomplete
Former existence so close it burns like the mouth that
Closes down over all your effort like the moment
Of death, but stays, raging and burning the design of
Its intentions into the house of your brain, until
You wake up alone, the certainty that it
Wasn't a dream your only clue to why the walls
Are turning on you and why the windows no longer speak
Of time but are themselves, transparent guardians you
Invented for what there was to hide. Which has now
Grown up, or moved away, as a jewel
Exists when there is no one to look at it, and this
Existence saps your own. Perhaps you are being kept here
Only so that somewhere else the peculiar light of someone's
Purpose can blaze unexpectedly in the acute
Angles of the rooms. It is not a question, then,
Of having not lived in vain. What is meant is that this distant
Image of you, the way you really are, is the test
Of how you see yourself, and regardless of whether or not
You hesitate, it may be assumed that you have won, that this
Wooden and external representation
Returns the full echo of what you meant
With nothing left over, from that circumference now alight
With ex-possibilities become present fact, and you
Must wear them like clothing, moving in the shadow of
Your single and twin existence, waking in intact
Appreciation of it, while morning is still and before the body
Is changed by the faces of evening.

The Task

They are preparing to begin again:
Problems, new pennant up the flagpole
In a predicated romance.

About the time the sun begins to cut laterally across
The western hemisphere with its shadows, its carnival echoes,
The fugitive lands crowd under separate names.
It is the blankness that succeeds gaiety, and Everyman must
    depart
Out there into stranded night, for his destiny
Is to return unfruitful out of the lightness
That passing time evokes. It was only
Cloud-castles, adept to seize the past
And possess it, through hurting. And the way is clear
Now for linear acting into that time
In whose corrosive mass he first discovered how to breathe.

Just look at the filth you've made,
See what you've done.
Yet if these are regrets they stir only lightly
The children playing after supper,
Promise of the pillow and so much in the night to come.
I plan to stay here a little while
For these are moments only, moments of insight,
And there are reaches to be attained,
A last level of anxiety that melts
In becoming, like miles under the pilgrim's feet.

Spring Day

The immense hope, and forbearance
Trailing out of night, to sidewalks of the day
Like air breathed into a paper city, exhaled
As night returns bringing doubts

That swarm around the sleeper's head
But are fended off with clubs and knives, so that morning
Installs again in cold hope
The air that was yesterday, is what you are,

In so many phases the head slips from the hand.
The tears ride freely, laughs or sobs:
What do they matter? There is free giving and taking;
The giant body relaxed as though beside a stream

Wakens to the force of it and has to recognize
The secret sweetness before it turns into life –
Sucked out of many exchanges, torn from the womb,
Disinterred before completely dead – and heaves

Its mountain-broad chest. 'They were long in coming,
Those others, and mattered so little that it slowed them
To almost nothing. They were presumed dead,
Their names honorably grafted on the landscape

To be a memory to men. Until today
We have been living in their shell.
Now we break forth like a river breaking through a dam,
Pausing over the puzzled, frightened plain,

And our further progress shall be terrible,
Turning fresh knives in the wounds
In that gulf of recreation, that bare canvas
As matter-of-fact as the traffic and the day's noise.'

The mountain stopped shaking; its body
Arched into its own contradiction, its enjoyment,
As far from us lights were put out, memories of boys and
    girls
Who walked here before the great change,

Before the air mirrored us,
Taking the opposite shape of our effort,
Its inseparable comment and corollary
But casting us further and further out.

Wha – what happened? You are with
The orange tree, so that its summer produce
Can go back to where we got it wrong, then drip gently
Into history, if it wants to. A page turned; we were

Just now floundering in the wind of its colossal death.
And whether it is Thursday, or the day is stormy,
With thunder and rain, or the birds attack each other,
We have rolled into another dream.

No use charging the barriers of that other:
It no longer exists. But you,
Gracious and growing thing, with those leaves like stars,
We shall soon give all our attention to you.

Plainness in Diversity

Silly girls your heads full of boys
There is a last sample of talk on the outer side
Your stand at last lifts to dumb evening.
It is reflected in the steep blue sides of the crater,
So much water shall wash over these our breaths
Yet shall remain unwashed at the end. The fine
Branches of the fir tree catch at it, ebbing.
Not on our planet is the destiny
That can make you one.

To be placed on the side of some mountain
Is the truer story, with the breath only
Coming in patches at first, and then the little spurt
The way a steam engine starts up eventually.
The sagas purposely ignore how better off it was next day,
The feeling in between the chapters, like fins.
There is so much they must say, and it is important
About all the swimming motions, and the way the hands
Came up out of the ocean with original fronds,
The famous arrow, the girls who came at dawn
To pay a visit to the young child, and how, when he grew
    up to be a man
The same restive ceremony replaced the limited years
    between,
Only now he was old, and forced to begin the journey to the
    sun.

Soonest Mended

Barely tolerated, living on the margin
In our technological society, we were always having to be
    rescued
On the brink of destruction, like heroines in *Orlando Furioso*
Before it was time to start all over again.
There would be thunder in the bushes, a rustling of coils,
And Angelica, in the Ingres painting, was considering
The colorful but small monster near her toe, as though
    wondering whether forgetting
The whole thing might not, in the end, be the only solution.
And then there always came a time when
Happy Hooligan in his rusted green automobile
Came plowing down the course, just to make sure everything
    was O.K.,
Only by that time we were in another chapter and confused
About how to receive this latest piece of information.
Was it information? Weren't we rather acting this out
For someone else's benefit, thoughts in a mind
With room enough and to spare for our little problems (so
    they began to seem),
Our daily quandary about food and the rent and bills to be
    paid?
To reduce all this to a small variant,
To step free at last, minuscule on the gigantic plateau –
This was our ambition: to be small and clear and free.
Alas, the summer's energy wanes quickly,
A moment and it is gone. And no longer
May we make the necessary arrangements, simple as they are.
Our star was brighter perhaps when it had water in it.
Now there is no question even of that, but only

Of holding on to the hard earth so as not to get thrown off,
With an occasional dream, a vision: a robin flies across
The upper corner of the window, you brush your hair away
And cannot quite see, or a wound will flash
Against the sweet faces of the others, something like:
This is what you wanted to hear, so why
Did you think of listening to something else? We are all
    talkers
It is true, but underneath the talk lies
The moving and not wanting to be moved, the loose
Meaning, untidy and simple like a threshing floor.

These then were some hazards of the course,
Yet though we knew the course *was* hazards and nothing else
It was still a shock when, almost a quarter of a century later,
The clarity of the rules dawned on you for the first time.
They were the players, and we who had struggled at the game
Were merely spectators, though subject to its vicissitudes
And moving with it out of the tearful stadium, borne on
    shoulders, at last.
Night after night this message returns, repeated
In the flickering bulbs of the sky, raised past us, taken away
    from us,
Yet ours over and over until the end that is past truth,
The being of our sentences, in the climate that fostered them,
Not ours to own, like a book, but to be with, and sometimes
To be without, alone and desperate.
But the fantasy makes it ours, a kind of fence-sitting
Raised to the level of an esthetic ideal. These were moments,
    years,
Solid with reality, faces, namable events, kisses, heroic acts,
But like the friendly beginning of a geometrical progression
Not too reassuring, as though meaning could be cast aside
    some day

When it had been outgrown. Better, you said, to stay
    cowering
Like this in the early lessons, since the promise of learning
Is a delusion, and I agreed, adding that
Tomorrow would alter the sense of what had already been
    learned,
That the learning process is extended in this way, so that
    from this standpoint
None of us ever graduates from college,
For time is an emulsion, and probably thinking not to grow up
Is the brightest kind of maturity for us, right now at any rate.
And you see, both of us were right, though nothing
Has somehow come to nothing; the avatars
Of our conforming to the rules and living
Around the home have made – well, in a sense, 'good
    citizens' of us,
Brushing the teeth and all that, and learning to accept
The charity of the hard moments as they are doled out,
For this is action, this not being sure, this careless
Preparing, sowing the seeds crooked in the furrow,
Making ready to forget, and always coming back
To the mooring of starting out, that day so long ago.

Summer

There is that sound like the wind
Forgetting in the branches that means something
Nobody can translate. And there is the sobering 'later on',
When you consider what a thing meant, and put it down.

For the time being the shadow is ample
And hardly seen, divided among the twigs of a tree,
The trees of a forest, just as life is divided up
Between you and me, and among all the others out there.

And the thinning-out phase follows
The period of reflection. And suddenly, to be dying
Is not a little or mean or cheap thing,
Only wearying, the heat unbearable,

And also the little mindless constructions put upon
Our fantasies of what we did: summer, the ball of pine
        needles,
The loose fates serving our acts, with token smiles,
Carrying out their instructions too accurately –

Too late to cancel them now – and winter, the twitter
Of cold stars at the pane, that describes with broad gestures
This state of being that is not so big after all.
Summer involves going down as a steep flight of steps

To a narrow ledge over the water. Is this it, then,
This iron comfort, these reasonable taboos,
Or did you mean it when you stopped? And the face
Resembles yours, the one reflected in the water.

JOHN ASHBERY

It Was Raining in the Capital

It was raining in the capital
And for many days and nights
The one they called the Aquarian
Had stayed alone with her delight.

What with the winter and its business
It had fallen to one side
And she had only recently picked it up
Where the other had died.

Between the pages of the newspaper
It smiled like a face.
Next to the drugstore on the corner
It looked to another place.

Or it would just hang around
Like sullen clouds over the sun.
But – this was the point – it was real
To her and to everyone.

For spring had entered the capital
Walking on gigantic feet.
The smell of witch hazel indoors
Changed to narcissus in the street.

She thought she had seen all this before:
Bundles of new, fresh flowers,
All changing, pressing upward
To the distant office towers.

Until now nothing had been easy,
Hemmed in by all that shit –
Horseshit, dogshit, birdshit, manshit –
Yes, she remembered having said it,

Having spoken in that way, thinking
There could be no road ahead,
Sobbing into the intractable presence of it
As one weeps alone in bed.

Its chamber was narrower than a seed
Yet when the doorbell rang
It reduced all that living to air
As '*kyrie eleison*' it sang.

Hearing that music he had once known
But now forgotten, the man,
The one who had waited casually in the dark
Turned to smile at the door's span.

He smiled and shrugged – a lesson
In the newspaper no longer
But fed by the ink and paper
Into a sign of something stronger

Who reads the news and takes the bus
Going to work each day
But who was never born of woman
Nor formed of the earth's clay.

Then what unholy bridegroom
Did the Aquarian foretell?
Or was such lively intelligence
Only the breath of hell?

It scarcely mattered at the moment
And it shall never matter at all
Since the moment will not be replaced
But stand, poised for its fall,

Forever. 'This is what my learning
Teaches,' the Aquarian said,
'To absorb life through the pores
For the life around you is dead.'

The sun came out in the capital
Just before it set.
The lovely death's head shone in the sky
As though these two had never met.

Variations, Calypso and Fugue on a
Theme of Ella Wheeler Wilcox

'For the pleasures of the many
May be ofttimes traced to one
As the hand that plants an acorn
Shelters armies from the sun.'
And in places where the annual rainfall is .0071 inches
What a pleasure to lie under the tree, to sit, stand, and get up
  under the tree!
Im wunderschönen Monat Mai
The feeling is of never wanting to leave the tree,
Of predominantly peace and relaxation.
Do you step out from under the shade a moment,
It is only to return with renewed expectation, of expectation
  fulfilled.
Insecurity be damned! There is something to all this, that
  will not elude us:
Growing up under the shade of friendly trees, with our
  brothers all around.
And truly, young adulthood was never like this:
Such delight, such consideration, such affirmation in the way
  the day goes 'round together.
Yes, the world goes 'round a good deal faster
When there are highlights on the lips, unspoken and true
  words in the heart,
And the hand keeps brushing away a strand of chestnut hair,
  only to have it fall back into place again.
But all good things must come to an end, and so one must
  move forward
Into the space left by one's conclusions. Is this growing
  old?

Well, it is a good experience, to divest oneself of some tested
    ideals, some old standbys,
And even finding nothing to put in their place is a good
    experience,
Preparing one, as it does, for the consternation that is to
    come.
But – and this is the gist of it – what if I dreamed it all,
The branches, the late afternoon sun,
The trusting camaraderie, the love that watered all,
Disappearing promptly down into the roots as it should?
For later in the vast gloom of cities, only there you learn
How the ideas were good only because they had to die,
Leaving you alone and skinless, a drawing by Vesalius.
This is what was meant, and toward which everything directs:
That the tree should shrivel in 120-degree heat, the acorns
Lie around on the worn earth like eyeballs, and the lead
    soldiers shrug and slink off.

So my youth was spent, underneath the trees
I always moved around with perfect ease

I voyaged to Paris at the age of ten
And met many prominent literary men

Gazing at the Alps was quite a sight
I felt the tears flow forth with all their might

A climb to the Acropolis meant a lot to me
I had read the Greek philosophers you see

In the Colosseum I thought my heart would burst
Thinking of all the victims who had been there first

On Mount Ararat's side I began to grow
Remembering the Flood there, so long ago

On the banks of the Ganges I stood in mud
And watched the water light up like blood

The Great Wall of China is really a thrill
It cleaves through the air like a silver pill

It was built by the hand of man for good or ill
Showing what he can do when he decides not to kill

But of all the sights that were seen by me
In the East or West, on land or sea,
The best was the place that is spelled H-O-M-E.

Now that once again I have achieved home
I shall forbear all further urge to roam

There is a hole of truth in the green earth's rug
Once you find it you are as snug as a bug

Maybe some do not like it quite as much as you
That isn't all you're going to do.

You must remember that it is yours
Which is why nobody is sending you flowers

This age-old truth I to thee impart
Act according to the dictates of your art

Because if you don't no one else is going to
And that person isn't likely to be you.

It is the wind that comes from afar
It is the truth of the farthest star

In all likelihood you will not need these
So take it easy and learn your ABC's

And trust in the dream that will never come true
'Cause that is the scheme that is best for you
And the gleam that is the most suitable too.

'MAKE MY DREAM COME TRUE.' This message,
set in 84-point Hobo type, startled in the morning editions of
the paper: the old, half-won security troubles the new pause.
And with the approach of the holidays, the present is clearly
here to stay: the big brass band of its particular moment's
consciousness invades the plazas and the narrow alleys. Three-
fourths of the houses in this city are on narrow stilts, finer
than a girl's wrists: it is largely a question of keeping one's
feet dry, and of privacy. In the morning you forget what the
punishment was. Probably it was something like eating a
pretzel or going into the back yard. Still, you can't tell. These
things could be a lot clearer without hurting anybody. But
it does not follow that such issues will produce the most
dynamic capital gains for you.

Friday. We are really missing you.

'The most suitable,' however, was not the one specially asked
for nor the one hanging around the lobby. It was just the one
asked after, day after day – what spilled over, claimed by the
spillway. The distinction of a dog, of how a dog walks. The
thought of a dog walking. No one ever referred to the incident
again. The case was officially closed. Maybe there were choruses
of silent gratitude, welling up in the spring night like a column
of cloud, reaching to the very rafters of the sky – but this was
their own business. The point is no ear ever heard them. Thus,
the incident, to call it by one of its names – choice, conduct,

absent-minded frown might be others – came to be not only as though it had never happened, but as though it never *could* have happened. Sealed into the wall of all that season's coming on. And thus, for a mere handful of people – roustabouts and degenerates, most of them – it became the only true version. Nothing else mattered. It was bread by morning and night, the dates falling listlessly from the trees – man, woman, child, festering glistering in a single orb. The reply to 'hello'.

> Pink purple and blue
> The way you used to do

The next two days passed oddly for Peter and Christine, and were among the most absorbing they had ever known. On the one hand, a vast open basin – or sea; on the other a narrow spit of land, terminating in a copse, with a few broken-down out-buildings lying here and there. It made no difference that the bey – b-e-y this time, oriental potentate – had ordained their release, there was this funny feeling that they should always be there, sustained by looks out over the ether, missing Mother and Alan and the others but really quiet, in a kind of activity that offers its own way of life, sunflower chained to the sun. Can it ever be resolved? Or are the forms of a person's thoughts controlled by inexorable laws, as in Dürer's Adam and Eve? So mutually exclusive, and so steep – Himalayas jammed side by side like New York apartment buildings. Oh the blame of it, the de-crescendo. My vice is worry. Forget it. The continual splitting up, the ear-shattering volumes of a polar ice-cap breaking up are just what you wanted. You've got it, so shut up.

> The crystal haze
> For days and days

Lots of sleep is an important factor, and rubbing the eyes.

Getting off the subway he suddenly felt hungry. He went into one place, a place he knew, and ordered a hamburger and a cup of coffee. He hadn't been in this neighborhood in a long time – not since he was a kid. He used to play stickball in the vacant lot across the street. Sometimes his bunch would get into a fight with some of the older boys, and he'd go home tired and bleeding. Most days were the same though. He'd say 'Hi' to the other kids and they'd say 'Hi' to him. Nice bunch of guys. Finally he decided to take a turn past the old grade school he'd attended as a kid. It was a rambling structure of yellow brick, now gone in seediness and shabbiness which the late-afternoon shadows mercifully softened. The gravel playground in front was choked with weeds. Large trees and shrubbery would do no harm flanking the main entrance. Time farted.

> The first shock rattles the cruets in their stand,
> The second rips the door from its hinges.

'My dear friend,' he said gently, 'you said you were Professor Hertz. You must pardon me if I say that the information startles and mystifies me. When you are stronger I have some questions to ask you, if you will be kind enough to answer them.'

No one was prepared for the man's answer to that apparently harmless statement.

Weak as he was, Gustavus Hertz raised himself on his elbow. He stared wildly about him, peering fearfully into the shadowy corners of the room.

'I will tell you nothing! Nothing, do you hear?' he shrieked. 'Go away! Go away!'

Song

The song tells us of our old way of living,
Of life in former times. Fragrance of florals,
How things merely ended when they ended,
Of beginning again into a sigh. Later

Some movement is reversed and the urgent masks
Speed toward a totally unexpected end
Like clocks out of control. Is this the gesture
That was meant, long ago, the curving in

Of frustrated denials, like jungle foliage
And the simplicity of the ending all to be let go
In quick, suffocating sweetness? The day
Puts toward a nothingness of sky

Its face of rusticated brick. Sooner or later,
The cars lament, the whole business will be hurled down.
Meanwhile we sit, scarcely daring to speak,
To breathe, as though this closeness cost us life.

The pretensions of a past will some day
Make it over into progress, a growing up,
As beautiful as a new history book
With uncut pages, unseen illustrations,

And the purpose of the many stops and starts will be made
    clear:
Backing into the old affair of not wanting to grow
Into the night, which becomes a house, a parting of the ways
Taking us far into sleep. A dumb love.

For John Clare

Kind of empty in the way it sees everything, the earth gets to its feet and salutes the sky. More of a success at it this time than most others it is. The feeling that the sky might be in the back of someone's mind. Then there is no telling how many there are. They grace everything – bush and tree – to take the roisterer's mind off his caroling – so it's like a smooth switch back. To what was aired in their previous conniption fit. There is so much to be seen everywhere that it's like not getting used to it, only there is so much it never feels new, never any different. You are standing looking at that building and you cannot take it all in, certain details are already hazy and the mind boggles. What will it all be like in five years' time when you try to remember? Will there have been boards in between the grass part and the edge of the street? As long as that couple is stopping to look in that window over there we cannot go. We feel like they have to tell us we can, but they never look our way and they are already gone, gone far into the future – the night of time. If we could look at a photograph of it and say there they are, they never really stopped but there they are. There is so much to be said, and on the surface of it very little gets said.

There ought to be room for more things, for a spreading out, like. Being immersed in the details of rock and field and slope – letting them come to you for once, and then meeting them halfway would be so much easier – if they took an ingenuous pride in being in one's blood. Alas, we perceive them if at all as those things that were meant to be put aside – costumes of the supporting actors or voice trilling at the end of a narrow enclosed street. You can do nothing with them. Not even offer to pay.

It is possible that finally, like coming to the end of a long, barely perceptible rise, there is mutual cohesion and interaction. The whole scene is fixed in your mind, the music all present, as though you could see each note as well as hear it. I say this because there is an uneasiness in things just now. Waiting for something to be over before you are forced to notice it. The pollarded trees scarcely bucking the wind – and yet it's keen, it makes you fall over. Clabbered sky. Seasons that pass with a rush. After all it's their time too – nothing says they aren't to make something of it. As for Jenny Wren, she cares, hopping about on her little twig like she was tryin' to tell us somethin', but that's just it, she couldn't even if she wanted to – dumb bird. But the others – and they in some way must know too – it would never occur to them to want to, even if they could take the first step of the terrible journey toward feeling somebody should act, that ends in utter confusion and hopelessness, east of the sun and west of the moon. So their comment is: 'No comment.' Meanwhile the whole history of probabilities is coming to life, starting in the upper left-hand corner, like a sail.

Sortes Vergilianae

You have been living now for a long time and there is nothing
    you do not know.
Perhaps something you read in the newspaper influenced you
    and that was very frequently.
They have left you to think along these lines and you have
    gone your own way because you guessed that
Under their hiding was the secret, casual as breath, betrayed
    for the asking.
Then the sky opened up, revealing much more than any of
    you were intended to know.
It is a strange thing how fast the growth is, almost as fast
    as the light from polar regions
Reflected off the arctic ice-cap in summer. When you know
    where it is heading
You have to follow it, though at a sadly reduced rate of
    speed,
Hence folly and idleness, raging at the confines of some
    miserable sunlit alley or court.
It is the nature of these people to embrace each other, they
    know no other kind but themselves.
Things pass quickly out of sight and the best is to be
    forgotten quickly
For it is wretchedness that endures, shedding its cancerous
    light on all it approaches:
Words spoken in the heat of passion, that might have been
    retracted in good time,
All good intentions, all that was arguable. These are stilled
    now, as the embrace in the hollow of its flux
And can never be revived except as perverse notations on an
    indisputable state of things,

As conduct in the past, vanished from the reckoning long
    before it was time.

Lately you've found the dull fevers still inflict their round,
    only they are unassimilable

Now that newness or importance has worn away. It is with
    us like day and night,

The surge upward through the grade-school positioning and
    bursting into soft gray blooms

Like vacuum-cleaner sweepings, the opulent fuzz of our
    cage, or like an excited insect

In nervous scrimmage for the head, etching its none-too-
    complex ordinances into the matter of the day.

Presently all will go off satisfied, leaving the millpond bare,
    a site for new picnics,

As they came, naked, to explore all the possible grounds on
    which exchanges could be set up.

It is 'No Fishing' in modest capital letters, and getting out
    from under the major weight of the thing

As it was being indoctrinated and dropped, heavy as a
    branch with apples,

And as it started to sigh, just before tumbling into your lap,
    chagrined and satisfied at the same time,

Knowing its day over and your patience only beginning,
    toward what marvels of speculation, auscultation,
    world-view,

Satisfied with the entourage. It is this blank carcass of
    whims and tentative afterthoughts

Which is being delivered into your hand like a letter some
    forty-odd years after the day it was posted.

Strange, isn't it, that the message makes some sense, if
    only a relative one in the larger context of message-
    receiving

That you will be called to account for just as the purpose of
    it is becoming plain,

Being one and the same with the day it set out, though you
    cannot imagine this.

There was a time when the words dug in, and you laughed
    and joked, accomplice

Of all the possibilities of their journey through the night and
    the stars, creature

Who looked to the abandonment of such archaic forms as
    these, and meanwhile

Supported them as the tools that made you. The rut became
    apparent only later

And by then it was too late to check such expansive aspects
    as what to do while waiting

For the others to show: unfortunately no pile of tattered
    magazines was in evidence,

Such dramas sleeping below the surface of the everyday
    machinery; besides

Quality is not given to everybody, and who are you to have
    been supposing you had it?

So the journey grew ever slower; the battlements of the city
    could now be discerned from afar

But meanwhile the water was giving out and malaria had
    decimated their ranks and undermined their morale,

You know the story, so that if turning back was unthinkable,
    so was victorious conquest of the great brazen gates.

Best perhaps to fold up right here, but even that was not to
    be granted.

Some days later in the pulsating of orchestras someone asked
    for a drink:

The music stopped and those who had been confidently
    counting the rhythms grew pale.

This is just a footnote, though a microcosmic one perhaps,
    to the greater curve

Of the elaboration; it asks no place in it, only insertion
    hors-texte as the invisible notion of how that day grew

From planisphere to heaven, and what part in it all the 'I'
    had, the insatiable researcher of learned trivia,
    bookworm,
And one who marched along with, 'made common cause',
    yet had neither the gumption nor the desire to trick the
    thing into happening,
Only long patience, as the star climbs and sinks, leaving
    illumination to the setting sun.

LEE HARWOOD

As Your Eyes Are Blue . . .

As your eyes are blue
you move me – and the thought of you –
I imitate you.
and cities apart   yet a roof grey with slates
or lead   the difference is little
and even you could say as much
through a foxtail of pain   even you

when the river beneath your window
was as much as I dream of.   loose change and
your shirt on the top of a chest-of-drawers
a mirror facing the ceiling and the light in a cupboard
left to burn all day   a dull yellow
probing the shadowy room   'what was it?'

'cancel the tickets' – a sleep talk
whose horrors razor a truth that can
walk with equal calm through palace rooms
chandeliers tinkling in the silence as winds batter the gardens
outside   formal lakes shuddering at the sight
of two lone walkers
                              of course this exaggerates
small groups of tourists appear and disappear
in an irregular rhythm of flowerbeds

you know even in the stillness of my kiss
that doors are opening in another apartment
on the other side of town   a shepherd grazing
his sheep through a village we know
high in the mountains the ski slopes thick with summer

    flowers
and the water-meadows below with narcissi
the back of your hand and –

a newly designed red bus drives quietly down Gower Street
a brilliant red   'how could I tell you . . .'
with such confusion
                    meetings disintegrating
and a general lack of purpose only too obvious
in the affairs of state
                  'yes, it was on a hot july day
with taxis gunning their motors on the throughway
a listless silence in the backrooms of Paris bookshops
why bother   one thing equal to another

dinner parties whose grandeur stops all conversation

but
    the afternoon sunlight which shone in
your eyes as you lay beside me watching for . . . –
we can neither remember – still shines as you
wait nervously by the window for the ordered taxi
to arrive   if only I could touch your naked shoulder
now   'but then . . .'

and the radio still playing the same
records I heard earlier today
                    – and still you move me
and the distance is nothing
'even you –

For John in the Mountains

In a mountain sun
pursued by my own phantoms
monsters lurking in the forest
                    in my head
an innocent forest out there
mountain flowers and meadows
the swirl of grass and pines hissing

at each open bush a terror
behind me   a dark snow
darker than your eyes'
dark snow
in which some flowers
can grow into me
a night when your river
could have left its bed
a desert awakening
a maniac pyramid
settle into a newness

your kiss holds such towns

Lausanne 26 July '65

a cat twining itself round a mountain-top
the mountain crying
tears set in the long black fur
a lake so cold
that palms keep their respectful distance
on hotel balconies overlooking this scene

this couldn't be
yet the cat's eyes – I know – have shone
in so many towns
shadowing me and so many others

if lions tigers forests could spring
from such an earth

and the train's restaurant-car with
knowing smiles exchanged over the wine
and signals so often repeated
that they've lost their meaning
and the response becomes a mere formality

dark woods with orange creatures
flitting through like forest rangers'
lanterns in the unending storm

but only repeating themselves
and other nights
and so lost again in the fur of nights
half-suffocated
but the plan always working out

and a head bursting from the lake
gasping
and catching breath
the submarine escape-hatch stuck
but a way round this difficulty was found
always given that last chance
when the pressure gets too much

so the idiot's grin and the calm return
of the sailors to their ship
and the mountain curling round the same
or another cat
in its well-meant and sadly clumsy fashion

That Evening Pierre Insisted That I Had Two Roast Pigeons at Dinner

The loon house woke up
it was as if in the late afternoon and the exercise was repeated
some days when the streets were overgrown
the odd mail coach got through and a
bear was sighted on the outskirts of the marsh town
your sentimentality is better now than
the earlier cynicism complaining at the
quality of omelettes

that solitary flag on the skyline and the
grey public buildings that surround the park
how you hated me but now we could embrace
it was and you saw it sunday papers
spread over your bed and my shy clumsy introduction
fleeing to another's arms usage can mean safety
I can tell this from photos
hasn't this battle field been too often re-visited

'hasn't this fool game gone on too long?'
we locked the hut up for the last time
and walked back down through the pine forest
the melting snow-line a thing of the past

Summer

these hot afternoons 'it's quite absurd' she whispered
sunlight stirring her cotton dress inside the darkness when
an afternoon room crashed not breaking a bone or flower.
a list of cities crumbled under riots and distant gun-fire
yet the stone buildings sparkle. It is not only
the artificial lakes in the parks . . . perhaps . . .
but various illusions of belonging fall with equal noise and
    regularity

how could they know, the office girls as well
'fancy falling for him . . .' and inherit a sickness
such legs fat and voluptuous . . . smiling to himself
the length of train journeys

the whole landscape of suburban railway tracks,
passive canals and coloured oil-refineries.
it could be worse –

at intervals messages got through
the senate was deserted all that summer
black unmarked airplanes would suddenly appear
and then leave the sky surprised at its quiet
'couldn't you bear my tongue in your mouth?'

skin so smooth in the golden half-light
I work through nervousness to a poor but
convincing appearance of bravery and independence

mexico crossed by railways. aztec ruins
finally demolished and used for spanning one more ravine

in a chain of mountain tunnels and viaducts
and not one tear to span her grief
to lick him in the final mad-house hysteria
of armour falling off, rivets flying in all directions like
    fire-crackers,
and the limp joy of the great break-down
which answers so many questions.
a series of lovers – but could you? –
all leading through the same door after the first hours
of confused ecstasies.
the dream woman who eats her lover.
would suffocation be an exaggeration of what really
    happens?
the man who forgets, leaving the shop
without his parcels, but meaning no harm.
'it's all a question of possession,
jealousy and . . .' the ability to torment,
the subtle bullying of night long talkings.
what artificial fruits can compare with this
and the wrecked potting-sheds that lie open
throughout the land? gorging their misery
and that of others . . . geranium flowers hacked off the plants
by gentlemen's canes and now limp on the gravel
paths wandering through empty lawns and shrubberies
afternoon bickerings on a quiet park bench while
families take tea at a convenient cafe, so nicely situated.

engines and greased axles clattering through the shunting-
    yards.
fluttering parasols running for cover
under the nearby elms as the first heavy sweet raindrops
lick the girls forehead. the slightly hysterical
conversations crowded beneath the leaking branches
waiting for the july thunder to pass. the damp heat

and discomfort of clothes. a tongue passing the length
of her clitoris . . . and back again . . .
erections in the musty pavilion which should lead to a lake
but doesn't. the resin scent and dry throat in the pine wood
across the meadows.

                    'surely you remember?'
but so long ago.

strawberries lining her lake in the dark woods
an old picture slowly fading on the wall
as if a flower too could change her face
as a dusk cloaks our loneliness

Landscape with 3 People

1

When the three horsemen rode in
you left me
there was no great pain at your leaving
if I am quite honest
you disappeared back into the house
and I mounted up and rode out with the men

It is strange that now many years later
aboard this whaler I should remember
your pink dress and the crash of the screen door

2

The roses tumbled down through the blue sky
and it was time for us to go out
Our horses were saddled and the peon waited patiently
The morning was still cool and quiet – a low
mist was still staring at our horses' hooves.
So we rode round the estate till 10 o'clock
– all was well.

Later at my desk – the accounts settled – I would
take a thin book of poems and read
till he brought me my dry martini
heavy ice cubes clattering in the tumbler
and vodka like sky-trailers gradually
accepting the vermouth and sky.
but this was a different ranch
and my dreams were too strong to forget

a previous summer. And what did it matter
that the excitement and boredom were both states
to be escaped except a grey lost and on
these mornings a ship would sink below the horizon
and winter covered the islands   a deserted beach

3

Once it was simpler, but in those
days people rarely left the city
It was quite enough to stand on the
shingle bank when the tide was out
and the sun was setting and workmen
would lean forward to switch on television sets

4

On winter evenings I would come across her by accident
standing in bookshops –
she would be staring into space dreaming
of – that I never knew

And most of this is far from true –
you know – we know so little
even on this trite level – but he – he was
more beautiful than any river

and I am cruel to myself because
of this and the indulgence it involves

I loved him and I loved her
and no understanding was offered
to the first citizen
when the ricks were burnt

The Late Poem

Today I got very excited when I read some
poems by Mallarmé and Edwin Denby, and later
in the evening, by F. T. Prince.
I don't get 'very excited' very often,
but today was an exception;
and the fact I got 'excited' was only
increased when I realized two of them – Denby
and Prince – are still alive and are probably
now asleep in their beds in nice apartments.

Ted Berrigan has met Edwin Denby.
I don't know anyone who's met F. T. Prince.
I wish I could meet F. T. Prince;
maybe I will one day, but it will have to be soon
as he must be getting old.

This poem is rather silly
but there is a place for silliness
even today when it rained
and was too cold for July.
It is a rather silly day,
in fact, it's damn stupid.

Do you really think it's worth getting angry
though

His July Return

'rushing to embrace we were
at last in each others arms
I kissed his ear
and the sun reflected in my
gold ring making it glow even more
as I gripped his wrist
I saw how much darker my hand
was than his
but with our arms round each others shoulders
there was no question of inequality

The public buildings sparkled white
and the green of the park could be touched'

When I had finished writing this, I looked at
my watch. It was 2.30 in the morning.
I decided to go to bed. The rain had
stopped and I could see, when I parted
the curtain, that the streets were completely
deserted.
Tomorrow tourists would ride in small pleasure boats
down the river. I would be at work.
But it is still worth considering what this
means to both of us, if anything,
though both our meeting and this poem
are not free from a note of triviality

I wish I had a cat

The Book

(4 Extracts)

I

It is so much a question of isolation and machines
and the systems never quite work out
and we're glad of it   or half-glad
through fear   the confusions when faced with 'logic'

'the nervous touch of sickly women'

and the motorcyclist started his machine and
putting the bike into gear left
and rode fast along the big highway
that led in a hard inflexible line to the
dock gates   drunken captains finally
sobering and breaking down with real tears
in the mahogany ward-room
while the chintz curtains were drawn by a fresh breeze
through an open port-hole and the heavy brass
catch glistened in the sunlight

'you're not fooling me or anyone else'

2

The 5.45 Pullman train, painted chocolate and cream, or
rather, nigger brown and cream, left Brighton station
on time as usual. It was october and dusk was just falling.
Autumn had taken the countryside and produced the
classic scene of woodlands whose leaves
slowly turned yellow.

The spire of the village church could
be seen behind the hill but we
had to hurry and so couldn't stop
this time. She drove the car
as fast as she could in silence
purposefully ignoring me. I
would have liked to have seen that
particular church – early Norman
has an innocence of its own.
It was the brown of the ploughed
fields, with rooks in the elms
and seagulls following the tractor,
it was . . .   No, you can't see
and the . . .   my contempt was equal
being a city-dweller by nature

3

The churchman was still leafing through his sermon
notes when the tea was brought, and even this
did not wholly distract him.

I sat opposite him trying to read your book
and, really, your poems have never had a better setting
than this. The staff of the restaurant-car were
discreet in the extreme. Their activities as
expected went unnoticed. Things went
accordingly and no real upset was allowed.

Our separation seemed only temporary

The main door was locked on that afternoon
but we were still able to walk round the churchyard
examining the inscriptions on the tombs. Later it rained.

I put down the book and carefully poured another cup of tea
avoiding spilling any
as on this section the track was very uneven
and the carriage rocked a great deal
The churchman was not so successful
but his minor irritation was only passing
I couldn't help but love him for this
and it seemed a reflection of my love for you
with your words still so close to me

The woodland outside at last disappeared
and then there was only the blackness broken
by the occasional orange light from a farm window

4

It was not the same and when the end was realized
with all its implications   I had grown calm

We had both avoided the logical sequence and were
glad of a breakdown in negotiations   The rest
would be taken care of –
imagined loves and the riverside farewells
are only left for our weaker moments
the tears and longing were real enough until
a corner was rounded to meet a new distraction

We parted at 1st Avenue and 51st Street – it was july.
Weating a cream-coloured suit and dark glasses
he crossed the street and then turned to wave – twice –
the lunch-time traffic was very heavy and I soon
lost sight of him.

The Separation

The time came when the desire to return
grew so strong that certain songs would automatically
    produce
the physical pain of real longing
just because they were markers of former street-days

the restraint was hard to bear
when the cold closed in for the year

when the thaw might come was a speculation
too distant to have much reality

The orchestra would come and go
and there seemed no regulation by which
one could plot or know their movements
yet at each appearance they never failed to chill
me with their blank faces and uncompromising playing
It was as though 'I' wasn't there,
as though it was all a self-supporting film
The leader of the orchestra would advance
towards me yet his eyes were set beyond me
It was so unbearable that I was forced to stay –
though the pleasure of mute acceptance was denied me
– their movements settled this
Many days were passed waiting in suspense for the next
appearance

When the sun shone you could see the cliffs
and seashore across
The little boats bobbed in the harbour

That the pain was doubly hard to bear since
it involved such self-restraint as to
not gulp down the remedy which was
a bottle with 'answer' crudely printed on the label –
the symbolism of this almost went too far

If a ticket was bought it could only mean one thing
and there waiting on the other shore
was a table loaded down with childish treats
and lots of cuddly bears romped all round the table
I had almost packed my knapsack
before I realized the spell might break

I had tooted the car-horn for almost half an hour
outside their new house before I realized
they might not want to come out

The old photo had faded and was now very worn
It was more than a matter of mere recognition

Yet underneath the forest even when the glacier
threatened imminent extinction
the desire to return to a warmer land
was as fierce as ever and no dangers
even in the form of pawnshop windows that displayed
neat rows of pistols and automatics – each with its neat blue
price tag hanging down so prettily – could deter me

It was a necessity to be continually reckoned with
even at the height of ecstasies
The ice-cold chewed deeper
It hurt when the 'answer' was realized
and the whole camp stood silent for a minute

The Argentine

I

Of course I was discontent with the ranch
the pampas was only there for one purpose
that the whole land knew of

The green continent groaned and stretched
while its brown rivers charged round in all directions
only to settle down as before
when the land fell asleep again

A single tree dominated the mountain top
but went no further than that

So many wrong and arrogant statements were
made in the geography books – and I
was not alone in resenting these

Brown chaos charged the towns and finally
smashed through into the very heart
of the people – they were terrified and some of
the people died too

'Can't you understand my difficulties?' was
whispered as I put my ear to the ground
'I wasn't prepared, and she could not wait
for ever' the voice went on and on
with an endless story

I kicked every door down in the house
but found no one

It was opportune that at this moment
the group of horsemen galloped into
the court-yard. I had seen them at this
same time last year – but this time
I was prepared to ride away with them.

2

This was not the first migration
nor would this country be in any way final –
the movement had been an agony dragged across
many lands   it was a well known process

The dead and numbed tundra or the sleepy estuary
with its brown banks and heavy jungle
'The grass was always greener on the other side'

She understood, I thought, that the ritual was grotesque
as it was necessary – and all this belonged elsewhere
just as the real love was elsewhere, but
this through accident and not desire

3

'He never visited the ranch' – and so in isolation
I continued as best I could. No profits were made
but neither were there any losses to talk of
What made it bearable was the memory – and hope –
an airport lounge with its automatic clock
and the milling crowds at the bus terminal . . .
He had a way of looking across a dinner table
– it at once commanded and yet asked for kindness.
Love and tenderness were the dominants – and the ceremony
of social acts was all that separated a fulfilment.

In fact pleasure was gained by the very anticipation,
by the polite dinner conversations and the easy talk
in the bars afterwards
The brief touch of his hand
or the caress of legs under a table
gave more than any previous experience

When these memories grew unbearable . . .
The mountains   the long ride and brief visits to other
      ranches
where nervousness made an evening pass quickly enough
in a series of laborious politenesses

On the way home, rain beating on the car roof
the essential notation of details like
the car's head-lamps and the night – their effect on one
      another
All this seized in weak desperation to distract
a realization, and sometimes even a regret

Such an image had been set so deep in my heart
that its destruction would inevitably cause
much more than local damage
and the fire chief didn't exaggerate when he said
'Keep all those people well clear. That building's
going to collapse any minute.
It's little more than a burnt-out shell'

4

How could the two see reality as far as it meant
the truth of their situation or rather how true
were their words and sensations – both come and go
quite rapidly after all.

On the sidewalk in Fifth Avenue just below 12th Street
3 men were parting outside the Cedar Bar
The older one had to go uptown – it was late –
and the 2 young men were
separately going to drift round the Village for a few hours
Then, as the taxi arrived, Joe reached up
and kissed John on the forehead.
The 3 split up. It was a hot June night – of course.

The second young man left outside this action
evidently felt something
It would seem that he was really the more concerned
with the older man and that he now regretted
his passiveness in that street, but he had had a reason
– though now it seemed a mistaken one.
He had feared to embarrass, where in fact a spontaneous
        act . . .

The frustration at a missed chance is universal
and a slight jealousy of the successful equally common
There were other days, and usually the older and the younger
        man
succeeded in gaining some degree of harmony

But . . .
the pressure of a train and a plane schedule
put a simple end to that development

Finding a torn letter left in a hotel room
he read – 'she must have felt something for me,
but I was torn in two,
and in the end I just waited for her to come to me
– and this got me nowhere, as she too had her fears
and I was not the only answer in that town.'

5

Mist rose from the marshes
and the rider was forced to skirt the estuary
and keep to the higher ground. Dew was heavy on
the coarse grass. The grazing lands stretched as far
as the eye could see in all directions.
And above this vast open countryside rose a hot sun
that soon thrust the mist back into the ground.

The cocks crowed and the horses grew restless
for the coming day's work. The dogs barked
and strained at their leashes as the first men
fed and watered the horses. This was the beginning . . .
Then midday.   Evening time   the faint sound of voices
from the other side of the yard

6

The rare view from the mountain pass
suddenly made everything seem clear
and the whole geography somehow too simple
The answers were obvious and the route through
all the country ahead

The journey had to be made and the horsemen were right
But the weight of possessions held onto,
if not for love of them, then for some sense of duty
and fear

These accounts of past and future journeys
became boring . . . and any violence that might have been
had now grown limp like the vase of dead flowers
that the efficient house-keeper will surely clear away

White

It all began so softly and white was the
colour that showed the most dominance
In fact – it was a glorious white
This meant that the toy soldiers had to all be rearranged;
confusion on all levels and 'no one was really prepared'
My arms were no longer tired – the rest had been good

It was a happy occasion
but you were so surprised to see the same flags still hanging
limply from the long balcony of the state apartments
In the end the ritual remains unaltered
and that too is comforting and like the 'last words'
of an important general's speech
talking of history, religion and tradition

The only sabotage was the irritating acts of open vanity
performed by women consciously or unconsciously

The paintings would have to be winter landscapes
and this means lots of white paint –
I've bought it for you already. he said 'look in that cupboard'

The New Start is near
and white is so tender anyway
like the little sail-boat in the large round pond

The Paintbox

What did you do? We all know how tired
you were, but you did, didn't you?
I mean the formula can be turned most ways
and it's only a matter then of local colour
to give *that* touch of distinction.
The surface then appeared different –
but under the paint?
Canvas was universal – everywhere.
The tubes of paint were so fat
and funny, as they didn't matter so much.
It was 'the rose mist floating down
on the white mountain crags'
that was in everyone's mind.
The poem was printed out like a neat label
and stuck below the picture.
We've been here before, haven't we?
Yes. And it's now one more poem.
That's funny, isn't it? or maybe
it's not so funny, but scarey instead.
I mean the whole routine of bare
canvas and the paints all squeezed out
on the palette and then it's just for someone
to step out and say 'Go' in a loud voice.
And the day goes by in slapping noises
as more and more paint is used up.

Sea Coves

Sea coves and cliffs, the deserted beach –
they all mean so little.
You are there and that is what it is.
The clumsiness of my actions.
We care for each other and love.
The sea is quiet and the streets
in the small port so narrow,
but somehow we get through.
It's only belief – what else
can words do? 'Love'.
This isn't a parable – the objects
are real enough. They have powers.
Allegories are in the past – there isn't
the luxury or time now.
This sounds brusque – what is the sound
of our love? The words collapse again.
That was weak, wasn't it?

I can't get my paints out now.
It's not the time. You know –
we both collapse, but somehow
it's as superficial as the waves
and the whole seascape.
We're here and stay put.
It's our move; we paint what we like
and do what we like
and all the words like 'somehow' and the
objects and the 'powers' are so little.
To talk of the plane now
would be unlucky – it's just there,

and the tarmac is so pretty with its oil slicks
and the orange wind-sock beside the white hangar.
'Yes, that sounds right, doesn't it?'
I do like oil slicks, but I love you.

When the Geography Was Fixed
(for Marian)

The distant hills are seen from the windows.
It is a quiet room, and the house is in a town
far from the capital.
The south-west province even now in spring
is warmer than the summer of the north.
The hills are set in their distance
from the town and that is where they'll stay.
At this time the colours are hard to name
since a whiteness infiltrates everything.
It could be dusk.
The memory and sound of chantings
is not so far away – it is only a matter
of the degree of veneer at that moment.
This is not always obvious and for many
undiscovered while their rhythm remains static.
It's all quite simple,
once past the door – and that's only a figure
of speech that's as clumsy as most symbols.
This formality is just a cover.

The hills and the room are both in
the white. The colours are here
inside us, I suppose. There's still a tower
on the skyline and it's getting more obscure.
When I say 'I love you' – that means
something. And what's in the past
I don't know any more – it was all ice-skating.
In the water a thick red cloud
unfurls upwards; at times it's almost orange.

A thin thread links something and there are
fingers and objects of superstition
seriously involved in this.

The canvas is so bare
that it hardly exists – though the painting
is quite ready for the gallery opening.
The clear droplets of water sparkle
and the orange-red cloud hangs quite seductively.

There is only one woman in the gallery now
who knows what's really happening on the canvas –
but she knew that already, and she
also instinctively avoided all explanations.
She liked the picture and somehow the delicate
hues of her complexion were reflected in it.
She was very beautiful and it soon became
obvious to everyone that the whole show
was only put on to praise her beauty.
Each painting would catch one of the colours
to be found in her skin and then play with it.
Though some critics found this delicacy
too precious a conceit, the landscape
was undeniable in its firmness
and the power that vibrated from the
colours chosen and used so carefully.

During the whole gallery-opening a record of primitive red
indian chants was played – and this music
seemed to come from the very distant hills
seen in every painting – their distance was
no longer fixed and they came nearer.
But recognitions only came when all
the veneer was stripped off
and the inexplicable accepted in the whiteness.

Landscapes

The ridges either side of the valley
were covered in dark pine forest.
The ploughed hill sides were red,
and the pastures were very green.
Constable's landscape entitled 'Weymouth'
is always in my mind at such times;
my memory of this small part of the
National Gallery surprises even me,
and maybe only I know how inevitable it all is.
The horsemen are riding through the forest
and at dusk they will halt on its edge
and then, after checking their instructions, ride carefully
down into the valley – delicately picking their way
through the small wood and fording the shallow river.
From then on it is not very far
to their destination. We both know this.

Somehow the action has at last gone beyond
the painting and this is for real.
But there can be no self-flattery on this account
– it has all been decided for us.
The illusions of freedom are at last
shown to be so obviously ridiculous that
most people cry at this point.

What is left is a canvas and paints
and a little time for distraction before the event.
It is not so much a justification – but saying
'Good-bye' now appears irrelevant.

All the lists and secret worlds have now been
exposed – there is little left to say.
'I did care, and the love I claimed
was and still is the miracle that continues
to astonish me. I love you.
It is only that death has forced
me into obeying its commands.
I am powerless and in its power.'
And that's a personal statement and as true
and honest as I can force the words to be.

The saddles creak and it's almost dusk.
It doesn't really matter whether this is
the real or a symbol – the end's the same.

Question of Geography

Facing the house   the line of hills
across the valley   a river somewhere
hidden from view   the thickets there
I can't remember   the colours
green   a rich brown   as the sun shone
turned to slate grey   at times a soft blue smudge
with dusk or rain clouds   the details obscured
but like a long ridge setting the skyline
Months gone by   the seasons now almost full circle

It was spring and our garden was thick with
primroses
Each morning I would go out and . . .

Ridge in the distance   everything the same
as before   it must be
The moors edged with pine woods
in the south-west province   a repetition
but the cathedral town unchanged
It makes no difference who was there
all inevitably reduced to the question of
geography or memory

And now awaiting the next spring
set in yet another place   this too with
its own colours and forms
the others seeming somehow irrelevant in the present
    excitement
but still real like a very sure background
– you paint over the picture and start on
the new one   but all the same it's still there
beneath the fresh plains of colour

The 'Utopia'

The table was filled with many objects

The wild tribesmen in the hills,
whose very robes were decorated with designs
of a strangeness and upsetting beauty
that went much further than the richly coloured silks
embroidered there could ever suggest; . . .

There were piles of books, yet each one
was of a different size and binding.
The leathers were so finely dyed. The blues
and purples, contrasting with the deceptive simplicity
of the 'natural' tans.
And this prism and arrangement of colours
cannot be set down – the fresh arrangements
and angles possible can only point through a door
to the word 'infinite' made of white puffy clouds
floating high in a blue summer sky;
this has been written there by a small airplane
that is now returning to its green landing field.

The table is very old and made of fine mahogany
polished by generations of servants.
And through the windows the summer blue skies
and white clouds spelling a puffy word.
And on the table the books and examples
of embroidery of the wild hill tribesmen
and many large and small objects – all of which
could not help but rouse a curiosity.

There are at times people in this room
– some go to the table – things are moved –
but the atmosphere here is always that of quiet and calm
– no one could disturb this.
And though the people are the only real threat,
they are all too well trained and aware
to ever introduce the least clumsiness
or disturbing element into the room.

At times it is hard to believe
what is before one's eyes –
there is no answer to this except the room itself,
and maybe the white clouds seen through the window.

No one in the house was sure of the frontiers
and the beautiful atlas gilded and bound with blue silk
was only of antiquarian interest and quite useless
for the new questions. The whole situation
was like a painting within a painting and
that within another and so on and so on –
until everyone had lost sight of their original landmarks.
The heath melted into the sky on the horizon.
And the questions of definition and contrast
only brought on a series of fruitless searches
and examinations that made everyone irritable and exhausted.

Once the surveyors had abandoned their project
the objects once more took over.
It would be false to deny the sigh of relief
there was when this happened and calm returned.

The bus bumped down the avenue
and ahead were the mountains and the woods
that burst into flower as spring settled.

The plan and the heavy revolver were all quite in keeping
with this, despite the apparent superficial
difference and clash of worlds –
there was really only one world.
It wasn't easy – admittedly – and someone
had to stay behind and . . .
The word in the sky had slowly dissolved
and was now nowhere to be seen.
But instead the sun was flooding the whole room
and everything took on a golden aura
– this meant we were even aware of the
band of horsemen now riding through the forest
that surrounded the valley.

The many details may appear evasive
but the purpose of the total was obvious
and uncompromising

The Doomed Fleet

1

The entire palace was deserted, just as was
the city, and all the villages along the 50 mile
route from the seaport to the capital.
It was not caused by famine or war –
'It was all my fault.'

The troops of desperate cavalry were ridiculous.
The naval guns could pick off
whatsoever their whim dictated,
but there was only one commander-in-chief.

2

The grey battleships lay in silence
anchored in the middle of the harbour.
They were ready all the time –
the only necessity in all this was decisions.
That may appear laughable – it's all
so simple.

The wounded was a subject never touched on
in the officers' mess. And the question of
occasional small but brutal outbreaks of
disease was similarly treated.

Nothing that could disturb the carefully planned
vanity was tolerated. That was the new order.

3

Grey waves slapped against the sides of
the iron grey battleships. Seabirds screeched
above the wind; they don't sing.
Even the ships appeared deserted, except
for the occasional dark figures that would
hurry along a deck and then disappear
through a hatch-way as abruptly as when they first
appeared. It was their continual menace,
however, that undeniably asserted their presence.
The menace. The power that vibrated
from the ships. The grey harbour.
Power. Menace. All terminals irrelevant.

In such a setting, it is not surprising
that tears or tenderness, shown by a small
but delicate gesture or caress, were of no consequence.

The men's minds were set –
they didn't understand 'pity'. The very word
had been deliberately deleted from all the books
scattered among the fleet. They needn't have feared.

4

With so few exits left . . .
'That was really ridiculous, wasn't it?'
Murder was just one of the expected events.
It would be carried out with the precision
of any naval operation and with the coldness.
Everyone knew their place and to disrupt the
series would be not so much reprehensible
as an admission of bad breeding in the extreme.

It was only actual closeness to the event
that allowed any levity. The midshipmen were
only boys, after all. And the officers and the men . . .?
– who is ever free from the fears and shadows
so firmly established in every childhood?
The point of 'safe return' had long since been passed.
There were no maps in existence
for this ocean, nor were there any charts
of seas, harbours or sheltered estuaries
where the least clue or news-item
might be found concerning 'The Successful
Voyage'.

Maybe they never did get there and, instead,
the whole expedition lay at the bottom.
This already begins to sound like a very bad boy's story.

5

Age began to show . . . and the divisions widen
and become even more resolute and rigid.
'What could have been' became altogether another story
like the family photos in the captain's wallet
– there was no room for sentimentality now.

The heavy service revolver seemed somehow too
melodramatic to be real enough for its purpose.
I suppose there was no doubt about efficiency
– only about motives. Wasn't this word
'melodramatic' something of a key?
How *real* was the death to be?
Was it an act of necessity or escape, or
one last weak self-justification, self-gratification, . . .?
The scene was, apart from superficial changes,

only too familiar, and tired.
The unwilling audience would at least be glad
of the concrete finality of this latest show.
It couldn't have much of a sequel, thank God.

The chart table was cluttered with empty coffee cups
and a haze of cigarette smoke filled the navigator's cabin.
It was very late at night, and the navigator
had fallen asleep, fully clothed and exhausted.
But even now, with so much unanswered and so much
    confusion,
there was in the atmosphere a feeling of finality
whose very grimness brought a strange joy
and relief. The death would not be that dark –
The dead body somehow would know a sweetness
that can be compared to the parable of the
bees' honey inside the dead lion's carcase.

The fleet steamed out beyond the point.
Nothing was free from the ridiculous and 'pain'.
The laughter was not disrespectful,
nor was it really that inappropriate.
The night sky was a dark blue and most stars visible.
Salt waves broke over the rusted iron decks.

Plato Was Right Though . . .

I

The empty house – the empty country – the empty sky.
Reverse it to A – B – C.

A: The large house
filled with many people – servants and guests –
it is now a country mansion.
It is white and has extensive grounds and woods.
There are many people.
They hunt and shoot. They laugh and talk.
In the evenings they play games.
It is all like a picture-book
that teaches vocabulary to foreigners –
each different object in the picture is numbered,
and below are the lists of words that correspond
to the many numbers. So – 12 is table;
5 : vase; 16: father . . . and so on.

B: The full country.
The map blocked out with the red of cities
– that's the agreed colour in the atlas key.
This continues into the 3rd dimension with
'concrete and neon' parodying themselves.
Countries, armies, 'The People' struggling with
'The People'. The borders on the map look
so pretty, with dotted lines in bright coloured inks
– all yellows and reds – dot dot dot – and in practice
nothing more glorious than a stretch of
ill-kept road with a line of battered poplars
one side and strands of barbed wire on the other.

The bad spy story continues. . . . The plot is very obvious
and stupid, even if it *is* all true.
No one could look at this and take it seriously.
And it wasn't just that the generals and borders
were ridiculous, but that the whole situation,
– including the very existence of the cities –
was wholly laughable.
The atlas became the one truly funny book,
and it did not escape our notice that what was portrayed
should be regarded in the same light.
To be totally 'negative' in believing the
countries as they were (and the cities) were
painfully absurd and grotesque seemed
perhaps the saner and more realistic.
It was a very pompous speech . . .

C: The sky was crowded with airplanes of all colours –
a totally unreal picture with dozens of
happy red, blue, orange and green
airplanes filling the sky in a mechanical
rainbow. Each plane, painted entirely in its
colour with no other markings, flies through a series
of aerobatic stunts, diving and climbing,
rolling over and over, and 'looping the loop'.
This is happening in a clear blue summer sky –
there has been no trace of a cloud all day.

2

All the previous locations are now impossible.
There is only this confusion in which no one
knows exactly what is going on.
The planes or the hesitating crowd on the lawns,
the house party going its usual way, –

but this only in a vacuum.
Outside is total darkness
dominated by the sure knowledge of Death
that takes on an almost human persona
and vibrates like the engines of an ocean liner at night
that can be felt many miles away and yet never seen.
(Black, as you know, is the negation of colour
and strictly it is not even a colour,
while White is all colours.)
And white is the love and only light that can be seen
to really exist besides the blackness.
The White is the only sure and real force
in an otherwise brutal chaos, and the only
home when all else has been lost.
(This new 'simplicity' was, in fact, a blessing
and advantage never before possessed, and that now
made the struggle easier and brought a sure belief
in the victory that before was confined to daydreams.)

A lone parachutist drifting down through the blue . . .
And even if he *is* shot dead in his harness
by the border guards, who really cares?
He has the same chances as anyone else.
'When you're facing death or junk, you're always on your
        own,
and that's exactly how it is,' he said. It became daily
more obvious that such clichéd truisms were only too true.

It is not a question of doubts or a lack of faith
in the forces of Good . . . but from this black and white
landscape, what is it that will finally be launched?
There is an obvious and reasonable impatience
at the slowness of the expedition to set out and,
at least, attempt an exploration . . . an examination

of what had happened in the past and what
could come out of the Interior afterwards.

3

The fact that there should be this co-existence
of opposites. . . . A desert, a barren plain, or,
to reduce this to its basic elements, a complete emptiness
    and darkness,
– faced by a crowded world of absurd objects
and events, and a tangled 'confusion'; and this portrayed
quite clearly in a desperate heaping-up of words
and pictures. The brightly coloured airplanes flying low
and at great speed over the countryside and approaching the
    towns
brought a wave of cold fear upon all who saw them,
that the jollity of the planes' appearance at first denied.

It was this fact, above all, that was finally realized –
and no matter how painful the realization, it had to be
    accepted
that what had gone on too long was due entirely
to a mental laziness that could live with this 'co-existence'.
There was no expedition to be expected or any news
of it to be eagerly awaited. If anything
was to be found or gained it would only come through
a 'personal action'.
        'All the necessary equipment was there.
I only had to dress and begin.
And it was not a matter of fierce lions from the story-book,
or navigating my sampan through a wild and thundering
    gorge
only to have to fight 300 Chinese rebels the other side
single-handed with only a revolver and my walking stick.

The fun of these jaunts was a thing of the past.
What it meant now was to live like anyone else
– getting up in the morning, washing, eating meals, . . .'

The convalescence, though once necessary,
was now over. All the wounds had healed and
the neat white scars could only be mementos.
This left no real excuses or causes for further delay.
'And the one simple and basic fact that love
had become a supreme power that radiated from me
was now the key to everything. And no matter how much
time would be needed, the struggle to deal with this
and other pressures was there and only waited to be
used. Like the quiet in the ship's engine-room,
this inactivity seemed wrong.'

For some reason the word 'LOVE' does not suggest
a strength, or grace, only a mild ineffectuality.
Yet beyond the romantic charades and the gaudy neon letters
outside the theatre – when the Real, and
the True essence is gained (or found), it's only this
love that creates a joy and happiness able to finally
dismiss a cruel haunting by Death and meet the 'World'.
And what the words and poems attempt degenerates into
     this –
a clumsy manifesto in which the words used
appear emptier than ever before and the atmosphere
more that of an intense but bad Sunday School.
——————————————PLATO was right to banish
poets from the Republic. Once they try to go beyond the
colours and shapes, they only ever fail, miserably –
some more gracefully than others.

In Bed

My teddybear leaps out into the morning
dawn is hardly here   the birds have only just begun
to sing   BUT he bursts forth with so much energy today
that I'm embarrassed to be with him
– his name is Larry, though I call him Joe.
The window is firmly shut as it's cold outside
but he opens it up and does deep breathing.
I curse, freeze, and curl into a small ball
– he will have to go.
'Dear Teddy Joe, please close the window,
there's a good bear' – to no avail.
Teddy Joe goes out the window
I curl up in bed and read your letter again
for the third time. 'Gosh, I do love you.'

Telescope

The army advanced by night
at dawn the pearl grey of the sea
a large bird flying too slowly   I may be tired now
but lying in bed watching thin white clouds
passing through the window in a clear sky
Your smile is inside me   I wait
In this morning stillness everything seems at peace
the white sheets   the delicate ring of my watch
ticking in a bare white room overlooking the sea
One direction the harbour and the green band of waves
below the horizon – the other the heavy roundness
of the hills, the darker green of the Downs
The army subsides and melts like the night at dawn
– it's in the past now. Thoughts of you glow inside me.
A pale late winter sunshine floods the whole landscape
in a harsh white light and so makes it
look totally bare – the word 'naked' can even be used now –
and this same air of nakedness in the sunlight
is like an announcement of the coming spring
The comparison expands and I see this all as a
reflection of your coming return that I now wait for
and how I lie here this morning thinking of you
Far from the shore a small cargo boat presses on
– from here its progress looks painfully slow
but this doesn't matter   neither I nor the boat's crew
can be ruffled with such good things so obviously in store
      for us

Return of the Native

The clouds descend so warm and heavy   again
A rigid number gives time to the day but with no
certainty except the recognition of being here before
Once more facing   being engulfed even
'I never thought it would be this good'   and consequently
sway held up by a soft 'greyness'   is that it?
eyes narrowing and the lids growing heavy too

There is piping music in the tents   the horses?
Can the stories ever be told once too often?
a new freshness radiates from the change perhaps

Slowly the clouds thin and . . .

The horses to be seen grazing far across the grasslands
dead zebras lying in the deep grass
and in the distance the roar of surf pounding some coastline

The giraffe is a bright gold

A wind flicking over the pages of this picture book
in which time seems to go backwards
'early lithography'   'pursued by furies'?
a volume bound in coarse blue cloth whose spine is so faded
the dust settling outlined against the shafts of sunlight
dividing the room
and all this despite various private emotions
whose relevance cuts only too deeply for those who . . .
looping-the-loop

'The tents have been cleared and there had been
no one there to leave even the simplest message with
So, starting from the very beginning again –
the menfolk sat round the fires examining their bodies for
    lice
and other parasites. Each success met with roars of approval.'
Closing the book

And on the return, after taking in the view from the window
once again, even praising its beauty,
yet all this more a formality than any fresh response –
an old lady's pilgrimage rather than JERUSALEM
    flashing

Reports continued to flood the warden's office –
throughout the entire district, on and off the Reservation,
carcasses of large and small game were being sighted
and in increasing numbers. The heavy clouds
no longer decorated a distant horizon – 'love you'
what does that mean?   in God's name in the distance –
they filled the air like snow-drifts
a soft 'greyness'   where WHITE had dazzled

The picture-book's colours had so easily drugged us
with their richness that only the vague glow of the present
backed with irrelevant and totally unreal dates suggesting
    history
appeared to exist until an unexpected gap in the clouds
revealed the proof of rumours once so quickly dismissed
It was not a matter of the odd death by accident
but of a whole bloody trail stretching back into the distance –
beasts trampling in their panic   'Irrecoverable Damage'
totally inadequate if ever a 'judgement' – and the time

unrepeatable and lost beyond the plodding repetition of
    cruelties

With dawn approaching, the birds singing in the darkness
– a young woman talks in her sleep, then laughs –
a happiness even in her dreams

New Zealand Outback

'The three horsemen' is written down in the book
You gave me the book   I love you
My great-grandfather, his brother and a friend
rode out and someone took their photo.
Snap.

It is Sunday and the scent of lilies
really floods the room. It is also a sultry afternoon
in summer.   I love you.
The picture-book is lying open on the table
and shows an engraving of a lily,
your poem about a lily and our love.

The three horsemen disappear over the horizon
I feel as confident as my great-grandfather
that I love you.
Snap.

Linen

waking on the purple sheets whose softness
The streets heavy with summer   the night thick with
    green leaves
drifting into sleep we lay
The dazzle of morning   the hot pavements
fruit markets   'The Avenues'

'You and I are pretty as the morning'

on the beaches
machine-gunning the fleeing army
the fighters coming in low 'at zero'
the sun behind them   and bombs falling all round
'Jah Jah'   CLICK CLICK   'Jah Jah'

the cheap pages crumbling already after so little time
St Petersburg renamed the Soviet Printing House maybe

you leave the town   'the softness' like a banner
though where
In the countryside the trees bare and scrub bushes
scattered in useless fields
the darkness of a stand of larches
called 'the dark woods' on no map

touching you   like the
and soft as
like the scent of flowers and
like an approaching festival
whose promise is failed through carelessness

The Monastery

The countryside rolls out as the story unfolds
Rupert Bear – my hero – is once more airborne
and flying his small and bright red mono-plane through the
    clouds
This time it's not Santa's castle, where the toys are made,
(you remember?), nor any other 'magic land' he's heading
    for
'Yes, *you* know where you're going, and I must envy you,
but then. . . .' There's some form of technicality
in all this   An obstruction, or holding back, maybe
Let's make a list of heros, I mean, . . .
      ONE: Rupert Bear
      TWO: Doctor Watson
      THREE: Sherlock Holmes
      FOUR: Kit Carson
      FIVE: John Dryden
There's more . . .

I find this silence too stiff and tense, in an awkward manner,
so then there only remains peace on 'the outside'
'It is difficult for all of us here'
Nor is it just a matter of the serene smile
or any of the other clichés, don't be mistaken
But cut down to 'good' and 'bad' – is that it?
The small silver cloud the size of a fist
that hovers before you then sinks into your breast?

'inside the harm is a clearing . . .'

There were clouds   the sky was heavy
the rivers were heavy with flood
The line of hills the mud green usual
after the thaw
Through the middle the glint of steel rails
In the valley is a small market town
almost a village

In the morning her white body
(it being north european) and the black hairs
Your desire is revived

There comes this desire
to be clean
This involves distance
There comes this decision
of the necessity
in moving
at the right time
in the right way

There are many steamers moored in the busy estuary
'Come here'   we lean over the rail
The town is a whole scatter of colours
Our clothes are immaculate and white

The kaleidoscope of the tropics yet the simplicity
As I bend to kiss you my lips brush your hair
Somewhere in the clearing

The clutter   Above the ridge
the colours heavy   washed through
and he said then
'every man to his junk-shop'
not moving but fixed
in those same games of 'identity'
Somehow a tight blue blanket
wraps us up
in the silly dreams
Your body

It's never like you dream it
turning this side and that

on the edge of town   the scattered houses
the Mill House roaring
people are walking through the water-meadows
it's a mild evening
we're taken in by the very aura
the famous cathedral
and the orchards on the hill-sides
this softness could be in any season

They're like running figures
seen as white flashes in the green distance
towards the rails

'Soon we'll be there   a few more days
you'll like it
the bungalow   the cool verandahs
and our walks in the evening
Naturally my work takes up most of the day
but it's only right that way'

We walk round the deck
the other passengers smile at us kindly
like accomplices in the dream
we all know

As we get under way
a cool breeze comes up river
and ruffles your hair

Central Park Zoo

(For Marian)

Looking at the zoo   the great white park
of a misty winter's afternoon   'You're great!
and I love you for it'
All the animals have their thick winter coats on
– the childish humour of this is so enjoyable –
A brass clock strikes the hour of three and
sets in motion mechanical chimes that are
beaten out by rampant bears and prancing monkeys
with heavy metal limbs jerking to the rhythm
– this obviously moves the crowd of children who're
watching – some laugh with 'joy', others gasp with
     'wonder'

Let's call this charming story 'A day at the zoo' –
all essays to be handed in by the end of the week

But back to the winter and coats
It's very crisp today and the air is clear
The *buffaloes* are magnificent and beautiful – they are a rich
     brown, and the hair is not matted as it was in summer
     'alas'
A pair of *bob cats* lie with their front paws round each
     others necks – like lovers – they lick each others
     fur (in turn) – it is a golden yellow
A pair of *badgers*
A pair of *lynx*
Two pairs of *racoons*
And the *grizzlies and polar bears* lie sleeping in the sun

Let's call this 'The Peaceable Kingdom: A Painterly
    Reference'
or 'Winter in the Zoo' or 'A Day at the Zoo'
In fact let's forget what we'll call this
Instead let's . . .   returning to

The zoo in the corner of the park
the white mist hanging over the trees
The fact we can become children again
shows how right we were in
believing in our love despite the canyon
which we entered stumbling along the dark bed
of the Bad Water river
But we climbed out the other side
though taken by surprise on topping the rim
never having realized the end was so very near
But there it was – the herd of buffalo
grazing on the lush plains
Geography in our sense *is* exciting
Plotting the whole course now
Sunlight and shadows of fast
moving clouds sliding across the grassland
I imagine North Texas   or even Dakota   Montana

'The end' only of this canyon   but a continuation
of something greater   compare it to a plateau
of great size and richness laced with gentle
deaths at its edges   the spirits of the tribe
waiting with a deep love for us
It's not so much of a descent either – but these
details can wait you see

'You're great!   and very wise'   we laugh as
we reach the top of the rock outcrop
'and I love you for it'

We flower   we continue from where we left off before
though the statement of this can only be
something secondary for us and therefore decorative
There's no worry
                    'People of the World, relax!'
We walk among the animals
        the cages upset you
When I really think I know you're always right
there's no worry   we're on the same planet
and so very lucky
that the poem should end like this
is very good

TOM RAWORTH

Not Under Holly or Green Boughs

(for David & Nicole)

the voices move.   they are walking.   it is time
it is time.   they are moving, walking
talking
       some thing faintly sweet
       the lemon drops
             dialogue

a pause they
speak in   place
     this is hans in front of
them and in the background they are held and
also in the movies

this is the banner.   music.   the whiskey
in the sunlight enters the water like gelatin   the gravel
white.   flags are frayed.   as she smiles the skin
tightens along her nose

             a record we save for certain days

in spain the garotte   twenty years
the woman said drawing the number large with her finger
a tightening screw, the lines got less   he
would keep them in a drawer in this new room

with the old stool
            years ago
a forecast of a present war.   this
is our job

                  gipsy on the packet moves through the smoke

the place was empty the stairs
had marks of old carpet the
aircraft's trail dispersed into cloud
he entered the car at the lights and gave me an apple

we passed the arch at seven
already in the sunlight the flame was invisible   a place
you can get a drink at any time.   here
the garden is thick with weeds.   dandelions
buttercups.   yellow.   we tilt back our heads
they have stopped.   they are looking

Sing

a certain
drum beat   it is that of
skin

the button found
still
    vibrating

produce
the body   this
small thing?

i hold, here
only the fat remaining   sound
of a fingertip lighter
without ring   it

is the pressure of air i
don't remember

Bitter Moon Dances

1   to start

waking and misreading my watch – nostalgia? – suddenly i
    felt at home again, gunfire in the night
the dream lasted an hour in the dream an hour passed –
    i woke again wondering what graham mackintosh
    looked like
hold my hand – i feel lonely now – cries cries they lie on the
    floor the cat disturbs them
kitten i tried to drown holding it under the water – it moved
    in the palm of my hand sound rising with the bubbles –
    a power i didn't want
sometimes it comes ready in pieces – sometimes i have to try
    and tap it like this, spraying out words to keep the
    thread from breaking
camouflage was the other thing i suddenly felt at home with
bitter moon dances a phrase we overheard
it was her cheek i kissed and the inside of her arm warm –
    this hand

2   the voyage – translate these sentences

it was the 21st october when we arrived at the capital
the guide was showing the tourists the most important
    monuments in the city
first we went to a rather big factory and later to a smaller one
i arrived at 4.30 in the train from malaga and stayed 3 hours
it was just striking 6 when we went to look at the city

3   the indian problem

16,000,000 catlin said and the estimate is now some hundred
      thousands
the later map shows how they were pushed west

Anniversary

the train runs, trying to reach the end of the darkness

for the time that is left, if you will permit
i will recant and withdraw from my insecurity
see, i give you this bullet with my name on it
how neatly it fits your mouth.   certainly
the words that trigger it are unknown to both of us
as yet.   i have worn channels in the air of this room
that are mine, a way of progressing
from desk to door to table.   just now not
thinking, i touched the tip of my cigarette
to the head of a moth walking by my paper knife
& realized only when it spun and spun and fluttered
what i had done.   a comet.   the patterns in the sky

the six of us move in the night
each carrying a different coloured torch

Wedding Day

noise of a ring sliding onto a finger

supposing he *did* say that?
we came by the front
sea fog twisting light above the pebbles
towards the cliffs towards the sea

i made this pact, intelligence
shall not replace intuition, sitting here
my hand cold on the typewriter
flicking the corner of the paper.   he

came from the toilet wearing
a suit, people
didn't recognize him, down the length of
corridor.   the room
was wooden, sunlight   we stood in a half circle

noise of two cine-cameras

i wonder what's wrong with her
face, she said, because
there's nothing wrong with it really   i
inhabit a place just to the left of that phrase.   from

a bath the father took champagne later
whiskey.   through the window we watched the frigate's
orange raft drifting to shore

i mean if you're taking *that*
attitude
        we rode in a train watching the dog move

noise of a bicycle freewheeling downhill

My Face Is My Own, I Thought

morning   he had gone
down to the village   a figure
she still recognized from his walk

nothing
          he had explained
is won by arguing   things are changed
only by power
                    and cunning ·   she still sat
meaning to ask what
did you say   ?   echo in her ears

he might have just finished speaking   so
waiting and
              taking the scissors
began to trim off the baby's fingers

She Said Bread, Fred

(for Race & Elizabeth)

in black & white
the cigarette end is silver

organ music, the women
in black
      (goza church EHV

                ree sunday
comerainorshine   she said a

fine day
we are passing the coast of africa
smell from the land of animals & hot wet leaves

i am dancing
yes, free
of this, they are
asking questions
eyes like a fly

      (you are two thousand miles away in malaya singing
      blue moon & i walk through the door & you
          smile &
      keep right on singing.   i

open the cupboard
in it lies the head i wore long ago when i was a soldier my
god, the rain on the night sea

Three

smell of shit when i lift him he knocks the book from my
    hand
i hold him up she pulls at my leg the other comes in with a
    book
he gives me his book picks up my book she pulls at his arm
       the other
is pulling my hair i put him down he pulls at my leg she
has taken my book from him and gives it to me i give him
       his book
give her an apple touch the other's hair and open the door

they go down the hall all carrying something

There Are Lime-Trees in Leaf on the Promenade
(for Ed & Helene)

the blossom blows
                    across the step
no moon.   night, the curtain moves

we had come back from seeing one friend in the week
they celebrated the twentieth anniversary of victory. fireworks
parades.   and all across the town the signs the french
people are not your allies mr johnson   who were
then, the old photographs.   garlanded the tanks with
flowers now
choke-cherry
               a poison   we came
separately home

the children were there
covered with pink blossoms like burned men   taking
the things they laughed
                              at the strange coins, tickets.   ran
around the house pointing up at the plane then
the only noise

there can be no dedication   all things in their way
are   the actual scars   tension.   the feeling
of isolation.   love
for me in one way is waiting for it to end

what to do? the woman, they said
lived on a boat   swans
built their nests behind the lockgates   the eggs

when the gates were opened
smashed.   each time in pairs the swans
would hunt out ducklings, and whilst one
held off the mother, would drown them
beating them under the water with their wings

we heard the phone ringing in the empty house then went
        to bed
later that morning we spoke for the first time

the sun just through the trees but still dark in the room
she with the hem of her dressing gown torn sitting at my desk
i looked at the things and touched them
                                waiting to hear the voices

we had come back from seeing one friend in the week
they celebrated the twentieth anniversary of victory.   now
speaking to them for the first time i thought of him
from that same country living in another place.   his tongue
he said, felt heavy now whenever he spoke english

there would not   perhaps   be time

saturday may 15th.   the sun higher   covered
with a faint sweat i read sun tzu
the art of war   'anger
may in time change to gladness.   vexation
may be succeeded by content,
                                but a kingdom
that once has been destroyed
can never come again into being; nor can the dead
ever be brought back to life.   hence the enlightened ruler
is heedful, and the good general full of caution'   i read
the wind blowing the blossoms in that week
two thousand four hundred and sixty five years after

The Dublin Zurich Express

so many things
i might almost go to them i
lean over the table
eating now
not thinking
crushing cigarette packets
end here? in this room
endless like
xavier?

i wonder what's happening outside
look out the window but *then* for
example i'd have to fetch
a chair, climb on the table
no. stop here.
demand some kind of treatment this
crying is a bit worrying

understand my predicament
now i have got here there are two paths
no decisions, stop now.
i see my lines
not
growing poems but a notebook for prose

TOM RAWORTH

For Paul Dorn

you said i
will not be here then

(the difficulties of packing   how
to move that enormous box

i noticed the shelves
were warping   on the knots
the sap was sticky

you still talked &
following your gestures from memory
i argued

(in the ashtray an apple core a
spoon with milk skin

the window didn't shut tight &
it rained
        you moved the cups

from the wall a bull watched us

Six Days

monday

i was alone then looking at the picture of a child with the
    same birthday
a key turned in another lock there was a noise through the
    window
the cigarette made noises like a cheap firework
in the ruins of so much love in this room i must leave
    something
the morning was sunny it is easier to die on such a day a
    blister under your foot and easier still to mention it
a need to explain this and a french dictionary i worried how
    to carry the bottle in my case with only a cork
sweat dripped from my nose in the picture a man wrote in a
    room behind a peacock there were two clocks in the
    room and two watches twenty nine bottles four of them
    my own
i wanted to share everything and keep myself it would not
    work
on the door a drawing of a lion in this room on the mirror in
    soap it said *write*
the plane was always level and the moon dipped

i had cleaned the room all my taste had gone the whiskey
    tasted like milk chocolate
i had bought all the books for my friends my shoulder still
    ached from the case i would be carrying more back
a leaf i had found and given to her all green with four brown
    eyes

five years ago i had stood on those steps the next month she
  was wearing a white dress the car was late i combed
  my hair in a window in the tube it was still summer i
was and still am addicted to self-pity

a handkerchief to my face and the blood dried i would have
  left it
the shelter smelled of earth there was a shovel inside to dig
  yourself out nine paving stones in the path
a tall brown girl in jeans who came up the steps of the bridge
  something about rhythm the line and breathing
motions

tuesday

the whiskey began to taste like whiskey the cigarettes still
  made noises
i had not noticed that beside the peacock was a quieter bird
  in front of it a dish and thru the window a countryside
day of daniel there had been noise and i fitted a lock to my
  door
a long while ago i read silone 'i came home,' he said, when
  he was able to continue
'and told my parents the doctor had advised me to return to
  my native climate'.

so wrote to you this letter
my jacket was wet from the window it was all grey except
  for one green tree by the pantheon
there was a sound of water in the streets the americans wore
  white trousers and red shirts
i counted my money it was tuesday i ate salt because i was
  still sweating
then the rain stopped and it was all white the tree vanished
  there were red tiles

he was five and he said to me why are you not nice look i
    gave you that calendar
i bought him a toy french car every year he looked after
    them and never lost the tires
i was aware of having a family the policemen all had
    mustaches
bought oranges and chocolate, bread, wine and coca-cola
soda à base d'extraits végétaux
i could not write anything without repeatedly using i
    someday
i would get over it
my teeth ached from politeness it felt like october '62

they take up the cobbles and re-lay them in the same pattern
they wear blue jackets and blue trousers and blue caps
the stones are grey underneath is sand
they do this every year and wash the public buildings

let me tell you about the needles i said
isn't it the truth? you find them everywhere.   even in
    bay city.

wednesday

today it is warm and the americans wear blue nylon raincoats
it is with a 'c' she said shall i wait outside a skin formed on
    the soup
there were brown leaves already it was only july
and between the grey stones drifted green buds dead fish
    in the river

i have no love and therefore i have liberty it said on the wall
    and underneath with my key i scratched 'lincoln'

pas lincoln she said bien sûr i answered an elastic band floated
     by
there are statues of all the queens of france she said there was
     cream on her nose
my throat is sorry do not go down those alleys at night there
     are thieves and murderers
this cinema is the biggest in europe maurice thorez est mort
enregistrez un disque a way to send letters

when we left ravensbruck she said we could not stop
     laughing and joking for half an hour

thursday

in the musée national d'art moderne there are three modigliani
     paintings two sculptures a copy of matisse's book
     'jazz' five statues by germaine richier a plaster
     construction to walk inside statues by arp a restaurant
     and a reconstruction of brancusi's studio
it was half past three the girl in the american express looked
     sad and shook her head
everyone was kissing it was like a commercial for paris
on a newstand i read in the guardian about the strike they
     said at the british council library mr ball has left?
in les lettres nouvelles june 1960 i read requiem spontané
     pour l'indien d'amérique with a footnote saying little
     richard – jazzman célèbre
from a corner of his studio the stairs went up to nowhere
there was a blowlamp and an axe a pile of wood
i looked at myself in brancusi's mirror and it was round

friday

they were painting the outside of david's house white
30 rue madame i would not have recognized it
posters say tous à la mutualité avec pierre poujade
pigeon shit runs into apollinaire's left eye

the light through her sunglasses makes her eye look bruised
other pigeons coo a sound of water splashing men shovel the
    leaves as the yacht is thrown it moves
a blue balloon the carts stand there are cigarette ends in the
    gravel
wearing a black dress with green spots gold sandals an
    indian girl walks through the gardens reading a music
    manuscript

on the steps at night five spaniards singing *la bamba*
long r's and a noise like a cricket
she moves another chair to rest her feet

one spot of nail polish on her stocking little song you have
    been pushing behind my eyes all day

saturday

a letter came i felt very strange at gloucester road she said
    after you went and i had kisses from four people
i wanted to be there people move into church a door slams
    the car moves

i could not say i tried
i said i
could not   people have hair on the backs of their hands
what did we eat we ate sausage a stew

of onions tomatoes and courgettes below in the square they
    played boules
six men and a fair brown woman in a black dress

emptiness a taste of brass the holes in my head filled with
    warm sand
a scar beneath her left eye yellow bruises inside her elbows
in the *marais* we bought sweet cakes in the heat without
    shirts there were still tattooed numbers
birds walk inside the dry pool the flowers are dark and even
on the wooden floor the cup broke quickly calvados a faint
    smell of apples

looking at the etruscan statues in the louvre there is a green
    patina on my hands my expression has taken its final
    shape
everything becomes modern inside these cases there is
    nothing without touching

children crawl under the glass   things are reflected several
    times

The Blown Agent

her blue gown is taking the smoke
the dust on the hem of her blue gown
blue gown – that's nice

in the low corridors of the old school   that smell
and her blue gown, poor dog
all those years the cake had lasted
we collected the dust in a matchbook

immobile   the petals   the horizon   the the
lonely in the radio and no room to click my fingers
over my head   moon   moon

on a bicycle, after the cars had left, her blue gown, **going**

Ah the Poetry of Miss Parrot's Feet
Demonstrating the Tango

we were leaving on a journey by slow aeroplane
that was the weapon you had picked for our duel
flying above a gigantic playing-card (the five of spades)
from one corner to the other – our goal the gilt edge

this is a pretense (i quote your note), a cut, take the short way
because justice is what the victim of law knows is right
your stockings rasped in the silence, the engine stopped
and i wished it had been a ten of clubs with more landing
        space

it was a game in the air, flock wallpaper in the cockpit
outside feathers grew from metal, flapped, and we began to
        climb
from the mechanical smoothness to the motion of a howdah
i picked up the card, removed my goggles, and began to dance

Hot Day at the Races

in the bramble bush shelley slowly eats a lark's heart
we've had quite a bit of rain since you were here last
raw silk goes on soft ground (result of looking in the form
    book)
two foggy dell seven to two three ran
crouched, the blood drips on his knees
and horses pass

shelley knows where the rails end
did i tell you about the blinkered runners?

shelley is waiting with a crossbow for his rival, the jockey
all day he's watched the races from his bush
now, with eight and a half furlongs to go
raw silk at least four lengths back disputing third place
he takes aim

and horses pass

his rival, the jockey, soars in the air
and falls.   the lark's beak neatly pierces his eye

North Africa Breakdown

it was my desert army.   no fuss.   no incidents.
you just have to be patient with it.   take your time.
a child leaving a dirty black car (with running boards)
wearing a thick too large overcoat: grainy picture.
each night round the orange dial of the wireless.

or innocence.   oh renaissance.
a dutch island where horses pull to launch the lifeboat.
we are specifically ordered that there shall be no fast cars.
where can we go when we retire?

it was their deduction we were afraid of
so shall we try just once more?
nothing is too drastic when it comes to your son, eleanor.

and nothing works in this damn country.
no, it's not a bit like home.

Shoes

shoes come from leather leather
comes from cows come from milk no
no milk comes from cows come
from shoes baby shoes
              come
from there to here hear
the shoes of blind childrens shoes
shuffling tripping a blind child falls into a cement mixer
a deaf child is crushed by the ambulance racing to the blind
   child who is the child of some dumb man who makes shoes

that evening he cries over a piece of leather stained with milk
the tear marks make a pattern he tries to read to read
he wants to cut the leather into the shape of a gingerbread
     man

he wants very much to have his child back
to ride on the cows back

The Lonely Life of the Lighthouse Keeper

snow falling on the lemon trees
the cowboy shivering in his saddle
what patience required to make *models*!
goodbye, pablo, it's all in the cause of the revolution

he used to turn on just to gloat at the *pauses*

now for the slow movement

Inner Space

in an octagonal tower, five miles from the sea
he lives quietly with his books and doves
all walls are white, some days he wears
green spectacles, not reading

riffling the pages – low sounds of birds and their flying

holding to the use of familiar objects
in the light that is not quite

Sky

(for Ron Padgett)

of the burned building but the frame stays
my room was there, stopping the clouds from entering
and i was inside.   i opened the window – sky!
a skylight – blue again!   a trapdoor in the floor
saw the roof of an airplane passing under me

i somersaulted slowly in that room not touching anything
blind almonds falling

Tom Tom

awakening this morning by the baobab tree
the bright colours of my clothes fading
catarrh a slow trickle in the back of my throat

the animals whose names i know only in dialect
in this place as the day grows and the air vibrates

eyes nose and mouth the dark green of our statues
face of an ape the symbol of justice and death gone

gone chaka the welder of a thousand tribes

Four Haiku

1

slow cello music
pushing the velvet armchair
as the rain comes down

2

time under pressure
dawn, and the green butterflies
crossing the ice-cap

3

to the last ashes
a chance of being gentle
holding the knifeblade

4

the method signs off
measuring the depth of cause
in the case of grass

Lion Lion

the happy hunters are coming back
eager to be captured, to have someone unravel the knot
but nobody can understand the writing
in the book they found in the lions' lair

Travelling

1

cold feet   the rain drips into itself on its round trip
round heels

2

you liked the lions and you heard them roar
the word that is forgotten always shows
a medical kit – how can i thank you boys enough!
i couldn't live with myself if i didn't

3

anthea's eyes on the dark corde du roi
in my fantasy the car continues slowing down

4

my pig, painted with flowers, receives the money
ooo   ooo   ooo   (oo   oo   oo?)

First Man? On Mars

of celandine and bright water, not on this planet
zeppelin, zeppelin, it makes me cry
how i dressed you in my mind in edwardian clothes and
    met you for the first time
in the manner a little archaic   i ate it
the pans all we had left CUT an alien 'hand' CUT puzzled
    how to unscrew? the knob
velvet to your ankles white lace to your throat and around
    it a band (the
arrangements are so predictable

is it my metier to be a policeman? i wonder
the CUT right or left? CUT cut? *how many?*

the shadow i make outside is the first shadow this shape here
as i am in my head the total knowledge of earth.   what
    was it?
bright this way and that.   did it move?

i am william tell's most accurate shot, listening to your
    rustle
oh my!

archaic in your manners you curtsey.   yes
it is opening.   i race to remove your bright clothes
the arrangements are so alien.   it makes me eat it CUT
it ate me   i ate it?   i am it looks like home

The Plaza and the Flaming Orange Trees

lions sit at the door of their hut staring over the snow
by the radiator she suddenly sat down – 'daddy!'
what have i to do with this music?
the spinning and reversing tapes dispose of *that* (she knows
he didn't get the job – 'daddy?'

boy the poor are funny
and when a white man dies it tightens up
'you must sing for us!'   what – right now?

day the first indian reached the ocean and dust blew over the
       water
i unburdened myself to the compassionate face of a lion

Provence 1

in the morning there is opera, faïencerie
dance dance to break off the filter

singing songs he could not play on his teeth

edge edge dance dance
in the morning to opera along the cliff road

his teeth were the filter and filled
with gold

that would not take an edge the bark
whittled whittled into a tooth pick in mourning

Provence 2

so i rode to my lady's castle
horse stepping gently through screaming vines
the noise of our train filled the valley

my lady was sowing
sweep sweep of her arm
white seed slashed like water

oh my lady is brown, red
and crumbling on the green velour
smear of my seed   horse   stop

Provence 3

the tape of my mother does not have that high pitch
the ape swung from the high tree

crash of the door took my mother under the ape's arm
she spun over my daughter in the brown dust

Provence 4

stone or heart, the ashes surround my plate
the horse i ride on is dappled with leaves
that would break the skin.   i wait for the sound of a car
in the noise of the valley bringing a spoiled gift

Metaphysics of Magicians

grey lights of the train
waiting for lines
purcell and the branches dancing
twisted into the room

finger brushing opaque glass mosaic
perhaps the steel core is lost
night and the train crossing
another room and smaller again

heth is the chariot
crab lotus and amber
wed to a chair
guarded by mirrored facets

tree after tree of orange

the lines between them

South America

he is trying to write down a book he wrote years ago in his
    head
an empty candlestick on the windowsill   each morning
of his life he wakes in paris to the sound of vivaldi in summer
and finds the space programme fascinating since he still
    doesn't know
how radio works   as in the progress of art the aim is
    finally
to make rules the next generation can break more
    cleverly   this day
he has a letter from his father saying 'i have set my face
    as a flint
against a washbasin in the lavatory.   it seems to me
almost too absurd and sybaritic' how they still don't know
where power lies or how to effect change
he clings to a child's book called 'all my things' which says
ball (a picture of a ball) drum (a picture of a drum) book (a
    picture of a book)

all one evening he draws on his left arm with felt-tipped pens
an intricate pattern   feels how the pain does give
    protection
and in the morning finds faint repetitions on the sheets, the
    inside
of his thigh, his forehead   reaching this point
he sees that he has written pain for paint   and it works
    better

Claudette Colbert by Billy Wilder

run, do not walk, to the nearest exit
spain, or is democracy doomed
we regret that due to circumstances beyond our control
we are unable to bring you the cambridge crew trials

if you're counting my eyebrows
i can tell you there are two
i took your letter out and read it to the rabbits

describe the sinking ship
describe the sea at night
he lived happily ever after in the café magenta

how to preserve peaches
they're counting on you for intimate
personal stuff about hitler and his gang
it's a chance i wouldn't miss for anything in the
wait in holland for
instance watching the windmills
that's more than flash gordon ever did

all those bugles blowing
in the ears of a confused liberal
so long
pretty woman
wake me up at the part where he claims milwaukee

On the Third Floor and a Half

grains on a spoon
the barrage balloons
echo in the bay

a polite gesture with the tray
to let them pass
away with gentle movements

stirring into the foam
a train where they have changed
the destination plates

Adagio

you are dead old woman and dead your husband
a wet leaf in your mouth pulled cutting the tongue
what a loving glance he gave you
tall men carrying you walking like horses

The Explosive Harpoon

regis couldn't break the pistol
corridors of panes against which the grass buckles
frozen glass sprays from his fingertips
as the blood on the leaf runs (dissolves)

cybernetic pain give me grace
the pigeon sees nothing still
caps in your mind that explode for years

wind blows in her cheeks, apparently
now is a word i like and morning, morning now
you think with my voice and all
your factories are circled by yellow machinery

your arrow's point the other
as are areas only can understand

fires in the hole behind the heather
stream overgrown with grass the daisies at an angle
the immigrant arrives   his face contained the mix to now

our town has been taken by whales, and children ride on them
and the bird on the horse through the black flames

Joseph Saves His Brothers for Ever

1

they said they had both had dreams and did not know their
     meaning

recently ruined in the sixteenth century
i did not think of them for a long while

her finger squeaked on the pane

2
in three languages
the blue packet
for months without company
i had to
the next one
no contact
the right hand side

i am he you thought as lost

3
it's really a dry period
dials show through bodies
salt goes brown
the pilot realizes the earth is up

train the bird
who wouldn't

The University of Essex

(for John Barrell)

1. gone to lunch back in five minutes

night closed in on my letter of resignation
out in the square one of my threads had broken loose
the language i used was no and no
while the yellow still came through, the hammer and the
        drills

occasionally the metabolism alters
and lines no longer come express
waiting for you what muscles work me
which hold me down below my head?

it is a long coat and a van on the horizon
a bird that vanishes   the arabic
i learn from observation is how to break the line

(genius creates surprises: the metropolitan
police band singing 'bless this house'

as the filmed extractor fans inflate the house with steam

2. walking my back home

the wind
is the wind
is a no-vo-cain band

and the footstep
                    echoes

,

   have conjured *peo*ple

3.   ah, it all falls into place

when it was time what he had left became a tile
bodies held shaped by the pressure of air
were clipped to his attention by their gestures

my but we do have powerful muscles
each of us equal to gravity

or sunlight that forces our shadows
into the pieces of a fully interlocking puzzle

4.   good morning, he whispered

the horrors of the horses are the crows
the bird flies past the outside the library
many heels have trapped the same way
he tolls, he lapsed with the light from so many trees

check the pattern swerves with the back
the tree that holds the metal spiral staircase swings
aloft the hand removes a book and checked it
for death by glasses or the angle food descends

5. the broadcast

she turns me on she turns on me
that the view from the window is a lake
and silent cars are given the noise of flies dying in the heat
of the library   the grass outside goes brown
in my head behind my glasses behind the glass in the precinct
thus, too, they whisper in museums and banks

Going to the Zoo

shapes that come in the night
three tulips through my window
hair brushed in the next room

the black panther extends his leg
here is the site of the battle of maldon
mum   ee   mum   ee   mum   ee

the order is all things happening now
no way down through you float in the density
so sensitively turned on the animals

The Moon Upoon the Waters

(for Gordon Brotherston)

the green of days: the chimneys
alone: the green of days and the women
the whistle: the green of days: the feel of my nails
the whistle of me entering the poem through the chimneys
plural: i flow from the (each) fireplaces
the green of days: i barely reach the sill
the women's flecked nails: the definite article
i remove i and a colon from two lines above
the green of days barely reach the sill
i remove es from ices keep another i put the c here
the green of days barely reaches the sill
the beachball: dreaming 'the' dream
the dreamball we dance on the beach

gentlemen i am not doing my best
cold fingers pass over my eye (salt)
i flow under the beachball as green waves
which if it were vaves would contain
the picture (v) and the name (aves)
of knots: the beachball: the green sea
through the fireplaces spurting through the chimneys
the waves: the whales: the beachball on a seal
still: the green of days: the exit

Reverse Map

out of the dream in which she has gone
in a man's jacket and hat: through the streets
that were at once granada, the lawcourts
searching for a file or a book left with her
compelled to travel the same route
to complete the ritual each time.   she was not
in the room where the party was, now darkened
searching among the shelves: a green dress
night after night   'hello fink'
but in the other house: again travelling the route

the journey is always anti-clockwise
and the loneliness is there before awakening
it is a dream known to be dream
and can not bring a moment's satisfaction

Purely Personal

dawg put'n fleas 'n m'bed: well, evenin' draws in
red lamp: orange lamp: green lamp: cold (fill it in later)
'for the sun always shines in the country of the elephants'

all information is false
as light blows out the room after the slide performance
'n we're closer than we thought

tired and lonely here on the perimeter
tonight i couldn't give a fuck for anyone
all i see is black: you can recapture nothing

Notes of the Song/Ain't Gonna Stay in This Town Long

the face in the dream is a name in the paper
bicycle shop smells ('sometimes my brain sings')
ice crystals bleed: these songs are songs of love

the levels write: they say
please let me in: the lights go out
(sometimes my nails sing)

The White Lady

on the phone   meeting the white lady
smoke hangs solid in the cab   i speak to the driver
in spanish   the arrangements have been made

Your Number Is Up

colour t.v.
works in a drawer
colour t.v.

12.15 p.m. May 19th 1970

(for Kenneth Koch)

the government has explained the situation to us
pigeon in the beech tree

first a shoe shine then the whole wide world
Frank O'Hana

(the plane dropped in an effort

the government has explained the situation to us

pigeon in the beech tree
first a shoe shine then the whole wide world
Frank O'Hana

(the plane dropped in an effort

the government has explained the situation to us

pigeon in the beech tree first
a shoe shine then the whole wide world
Frank O'Hana

(the plane dropped in an effort

pigeon in the beech tree

the government has explained the situation to us
first a shoe shine then the whole wide world
Frank O'Hana

(the plane dropped in an effort

this vehicle is fitted with a hope anti jack knife device 1)2)3)4)

8.06 p.m. June 10th 1970

poem

PENGUIN MODERN POETS

*Not for sale in the U.S.A.
†Not for sale in the U.S.A. or Canada